Rocks: The Blind Guy

The author, Thomas P. Costell
York City on September 21, 1923. He grew up in the Country Club Road section of Pelham Bay Park, Bronx, New York. Mr. Costello served in World War II with the Third Infantry Division on the Anzio Beachhead, where he was taken as a prisoner by German forces. He spent one year and one week, as a Prisoner of War, and was liberated on V.E. Day by the American Army.

Mr. Costello attended Holy Cross College on a football scholarship and was quite happy when he scored a touch-down against Boston College, Holy Cross' arch rival that helped to win the game for Holy Cross. He graduated from Holy Cross College in 1948. He was voted as Class President that same year, and was chosen to give the valedictory oration for his class at the commencement exercises. He then went on to obtain his law degree and spent his professional life as an attorney.

Tom Costello was married to the late Anne Margaret McKeon of Worcester, Massachusetts. They had five children, ten grandchildren, and to date, five great grandchildren.

Rocks: The Blind Guy at the Lake

Ellen Pinkos Cobb, Editor, is an employment lawyer in Massachusetts, concentrating on employment discrimination and global workplace psychosocial issues such as bullying and stress. She is a graduate of Bowdoin College and the University of Connecticut School of Law.

Marianne Alice Quattrociocchi, Editor/Administrative Assistant, typed and edited the manuscript for the author, her father.

Rachel E. Rosenbaum, past President of The Carroll Center for the Blind, made this book possible.

Rocks: The Blind Guy at the Lake

Dedicated to "Frank and Lois Marshall,
Two Who Are One"

Dear Ursula & Family
This book of mine was recently published. It is about a blind class-mate of mine at Holy Cross College

I hope that you enjoy reading it

In my God bless you to the core of your hearts

Tomás Peadar Mac O Uisdealú

Rocks: The Blind Guy at the Lake

Rocks: The Blind Guy at the Lake

TABLE OF CONTENTS

Rocks: The Blind Guy at the Lake

Rocks: The Blind Guy at the Lake

The best and most

beautiful things

in the world cannot be

seen, nor touched, but

are felt in the heart.

Helen Keller

INTRODUCTION

The story of Bill Gallagher's life is not the story of just one blinded person. It is also the story of countless hundreds of thousands of other individuals who have been born blind or who were blinded after birth.

Just as Bill's journey in life was truly heroic, so are the journeys of countless others like him who have climbed the mountain of adversity and have been able to blend into a society in such a way that the sighted community became unaware of, or not conscious of, their blindness.

It is my hope that by telling Bill's story, the sighted community will come to a better understanding of the enormous challenge that confronts a blinded person and how the blinded person is able to cope with and adapt to the problem at hand.

Bill's life also illustrates how the sighted community has helped the blinded community and can help those who are blind to become an active part of the fabric of society. Giving care and comfort to one who is less fortunate ennobles both the one who gives and the one who receives.

--

Thomas Costello

In our sleep
Pain cannot forget
Falls drop by drop
And in our despair
Against our will
Comes wisdom
Through the awful
grace of God

Aeschylus

THE EARLY YEARS

On a lovely autumn day

In the year of '22

Our laughing boy

Came our welcome way.

From God a gift of joy

To all mankind

But especially, to the blind.

-Thomas P. Costello

William Francis Gallagher was born on October 30, 1922 in Maynard, Massachusetts, a small New England mill town located not far from Boston. Little did the world know then that this child, born in humble circumstances, would save countless thousands of blind and visually impaired people from a life of hopelessness and despair.

In the 1920s, Maynard was a blue-collar town with about seven thousand residents, most of them hard-working people who were not rich in material things. It was a town in which everyone knew each other and where everyone was always ready and willing to help a neighbor in need.

William, or Bill as most of his childhood friends called him, had two sisters—Mary, who was four years older than Bill, and Rita, who was a year and a half older. Their mother, Mary Ryan, had grown up in the town of Concord, near Maynard. When she was twelve years old she was orphaned, and went to live with her great aunt (her mother's father's sister) as there was no other family. She studied the art of homemaking at school and married Bill's father, William Gallagher, not long after she graduated from high school.

According to her older daughter, Mary Ryan made all of her children's clothes and was an excellent cook and housekeeper. Young Mary described her mother as being thoughtful and kind, "just a good person." Before she married, Mary worked as a maid for a wealthy family that wanted to adopt her. Their son was especially fond of her, but Mary's great aunt refused to consider any thought of adoption.

William worked in a woolen mill in Maynard and is described by his daughter Mary as being "very hard-working and most patient and kind." During the 1930s, the era of the Great Depression, there was little or no work at the mill. William Gallagher was forced to take any odd job he could find, including labor on local farms. Sometimes he held two or three part-time jobs at the same time, just to keep food on the table, according to his grandson Tom Sullivan, Rita's son. Mary often worked part time as a housekeeper to make ends meet.

His grandfather "never owned a car, never owned a house; he always rented," recalls Tom, who spent several summers with "Nanny" and "Paw" when he was a child. Sometimes, during the summer, Paw treated Tom and his brother Steve by taking them swimming or to a baseball game. In order to do so, he had to borrow a neighbor's car.

Since times were hard, adding Tom to the family for three months was not easy on his grandparents, but they both were generous people and shared everything they had.

Paw apparently had a special way with children. He spoke their language and got down to their level, playing cards and other games with them. A rabid Red Sox fan, he listened faithfully to the ball games on summer afternoons. Many a summer afternoon, Tom sat down with Paw, listening to the Red Sox games on radio. Tom recalls, "I looked up to Paw as much as anyone I know."

Rocks: The Blind Guy at the Lake

Tom recalls that Nanny was steady and dependable, the source of great strength and faith no matter what the adversity. He praises her as a wonderful individual: "She gave you most anything you wanted but never to spoil you."

****

Young Bill had a normal boyhood and was especially fond of playing baseball. When he was only thirteen or fourteen years old, he saved a young boy, only seven or eight years old, from drowning.

It was not long afterward, however, that tragedy struck and Bill's life was changed forever.

One morning when he was fifteen, he woke up and looked in the mirror, as usual. Bill later described that moment in these poignant words: "I looked in the mirror and I was not there."

Dr. Flaherty, the family physician, drove him to a specialist in Boston, but the cause of Bill's sudden blindness was never determined. His parents were devastated, but Bill's first thoughts were not for himself and his great loss. He did his best to cheer up his parents, saying "Mom, Dad, don't worry. Everything will be all right."

His sister Mary says that this reaction was very characteristic of Bill, who was "the best-natured person I ever met. It was unbelievable the way he accepted his blindness." She remembers that when he called her on the telephone in later years, he would always ask "How can I help you?" and never "How can you help me?" Tom Sullivan agrees. "Billy was able to handle any adversity that came his way, including the Parkinson's disease that he contracted toward the end of his life. He just plain accepted it and never complained or asked "Why me?"

Bill became especially close to his sister Rita after he became blind. She was his first reader, and whenever he wanted to go someplace, she would take him there. Their close relationship continued throughout their lives. (At one time, Rita had a Springer

Rocks: The Blind Guy at the Lake

Spaniel she called "Rocks" because the dog was indestructible.)

Because of their relationship, Rita's son Tom, born when Bill was 24 years old, also grew very close to his uncle and has many fond memories of times they spent together.

One of his favorite stories took place when Tom was in the eighth grade. He was working as a golf caddy at a local course, and as often happens with young caddies, he became a very good golfer. One day when his uncle Bill was visiting, he said to Tom: "I hear that you are a pretty good golfer. You know, I play that game myself." Tom was somewhat taken aback and thought to himself, "A blind man playing golf? Impossible!"

Bill must have heard him thinking, because he said to Tom: "You don't believe me, do you? Get a five iron out of your bag and a whiffle ball, which I know you must have, and we'll go out into the backyard and I'll show you my prowess." Tom did as he was instructed and out they went.

"We need a target, Tom," Bill said. "How about that oak tree?" Tom suggested.

"Good enough, my boy. Now follow these instructions. Line up my shoulders in such a way that they are in a direct line to the oak tree with my left shoulder the one closer to the tree. Put the whiffle ball down on the ground. Hand me the club and put the face of the club directly behind the ball. My feet should be spread apart the width of my shoulders."

"Alright," he continued, "My hands are gripping the club, and the club face is behind the ball. Am I properly aligned, Tom?"

"Yes, Uncle Bill."

Bill then took a nice easy, smooth swing and hit the ball flush. The ball hit the target dead center. Young Tom was astounded. They continued the exercise for several minutes. Once in a while, Bill would miss the target and he would reprimand Tom with a grin, "You didn't have me lined up correctly!"

Rocks: The Blind Guy at the Lake

As the years passed by, the friendship between Billy and Tom grew. When Rocks was working in Boston, Tom often went to visit him. Both of them enjoyed walking around Kenmore Square. On one occasion, Rocks took Tom's elbow and gave directions to his nephew to go to a certain destination in Boston. Tom felt Rocks pushing in his elbow, saying in effect, "Get moving, boy, get moving!"

When Tom was in the eighth grade, Rocks took him to a Celtics game in the old Boston Garden. After the game, Rocks took Tom into the Celtics locker room, where he met some of the greatest stars ever to play the game of basketball – Bob Cousy, Tommy Heinshon, Bill Russell, K.C. Jones and Sam Jones. No young boy ever had it any better than Tom did with his Uncle Bill. I asked Tom what he thought was Rocks' greatest accomplishment on a human level. Tom answered: "It was his uncanny ability to deal with another human being on a person-to-person level."

Tom and Bill also enjoyed going to the movies together. As they sat in the theater, Bill would listen to the dialogue and his nephew would describe the action on the screen. Not surprisingly, Tom says: "Whenever I was with Bill, I never felt that I was with a blind man."

PERKINS SCHOOL FOR THE BLIND

For several years after Bill became blind, he and his family hoped and prayed that his vision might return. When it became clear that this would never be the case, Bill was enrolled at the Perkins School for the Blind in Boston in 1941 to complete his high school education. As he himself later wrote, "Before enrolling at Perkins at age 18, I had been out of school for three years and had a great deal of catching up to do. I had no intention of going on for higher education; for one thing, my grades in public high school wouldn't have allowed it. At Perkins, however, I became interested in going to college and made arrangements, near the end of my senior year, to stay on for one more year and complete a postgraduate course to prepare me for college."

****

In 1829 Dr. John Fisher chartered the first school for the blind in the United States. Four years later, as enrollment grew, Thomas Perkins, vice president and a school trustee, offered his large home to the school to meet the growing demand for educational services for blind children. After several years, when the need for a still larger facility became apparent, Perkins sold his house and donated the proceeds so that the school might move to a former hotel in South Boston. In honor of his generosity, the school was named for him.

In 1842, when world-famous author Charles Dickens was traveling in America, he visited the school. So impressed was he with its work that he enthusiastically praised it in his book *American Notes*. Years later, in 1886, a woman in Alabama read Dickens's book, and felt a surge of possibility for her six-year-old daughter, deaf and blind since the age of nineteen months. Kate Adams Keller contacted the Perkins School with the hope that perhaps her daughter, Helen, could be educated. The director of the school sent Perkins graduate Anne Sullivan to Alabama to teach Helen Keller at her home. The following year, in 1888, Helen came with her teacher to the school, where they stayed until 1893. In 1956, more than 60 years later, Helen Keller returned to the school to dedicate the Keller-Sullivan building in memory of her beloved teacher.

In 1912 the school moved yet again to a thirty-eight-acre campus in Watertown, Massachusetts where it remains today. In 1944, nearly one hundred years after Dickens's visit, Bill Gallagher became a student there. Kevin Lessard, who worked at the school for many years before serving as president from 1984 to 2003, met Bill in the 1960s. Together they became active in finding ways to improve education and rehabilitation services for blind and multi-handicapped children and adults. "In addition to being a very good student," Mr. Lessard reports, "Bill was also very athletic and he was a very important and valuable member of the Perkins wrestling and football teams during his tenure at the school. Bill loved all sports, and served as president of the Athletic Association. Before he graduated from Perkins, Bill spent a considerable amount of time talking with teachers and the administration about continuing his higher education at a college that would have high academic requirements and that would also offer him an opportunity to follow their sports program." In addition to his involvement in sports, Bill was a member of the drama and debating societies. "In my estimation," adds Mr. Lessard, "Bill Gallagher ranks in the top tier of Perkins graduates who have made very significant contributions to the field of blindness throughout our country and around the world."

****

Some years ago while addressing a Rotary Club meeting, Bill Gallagher described a typical day at Perkins, where students ranged from four or five years old through senior year in high school:

The bell rings at 6:30 and breakfast is at 7:00. At a table five blind students are seated with two teachers who explain what [activities] they have for the day. ... After breakfast some return upstairs to make their beds and do chores. At 8:30 is chapel with singing of hymns, reading the Bible, and perhaps a talk on current events. The first class is at 9:00. For the first few weeks, students are guided to the classes; after that they are on their own. [When] out walking, the rule is: keep to the right. I wear leather heels so that when walking along I can tell whether it's sand, cement, or grass I am walking on.

In the English class, all the books are in Braille, and the classes are lectures or discussion periods. In an examination you use a typewriter or write in Braille. Next may be a manual training class to develop touch and use the hands as much as possible: caning, weaving, piano tuning, and such things are taught to enable the student [after he leaves school] to have a trade. Foreign languages, algebra, and other subjects are also taught.

At 4:30 is the recreation period. In the fall the students play touch football outdoors, often with four or five blind persons on a side and four or five partly blind. Some can catch a football or can make out dimly that an object is passing them. In winter, recreation consists of indoor things. Wrestling is popular, and wrestling competitions are held with public and private schools. In my senior year we won seven matches and lost one out of eight.

In summertime we have swimming, tumbling, and softball played with a large beach ball. The [sound of the] bounce gives the direction, which is good practice for a blind person.

Sometimes at 4:30 we put on plays. People like to come to Perkins to see blind people act. The students made money for the theater fund and saw plays for themselves or went to a symphony. Acting helps to correct the blind person's mannerisms or "blindisms."[i] It is good practice to pick up cues, to follow stage directions, to learn how far to stand away. A rug placed on the floor can give the actor a cue as to where to stand or kneel. Some blind people can distinguish color a little, and for them blue lights or a yellow scarf can help them fix their positions.

Music, concerts, and Glee Club offer enjoyment to those who are musically inclined. In the reading room, students work on their next day's assignments, reading Braille or playing records--talking books-- which include all the classical books and best sellers. Everyone had to learn to use the typewriter. I once wrote a four-page letter to a friend, who wrote back that he had received four blank pages. I forgot to make sure there was a ribbon in the typewriter!

In the evenings the students walk, drop in to the school cafeteria for an ice cream soda, or listen to the radio. At 10:00 or 10:30, lights are supposed to be out. But the blind can read in the dark, so they can continue to read or study as long as they wish without minding that the lights are out.

Following the school's comprehensive education, some students went on to college, others into teaching or music. Still others became piano tuners and lawyers. During the war they showed that people who were blind were capable of working in factories.

A person born blind or blinded at an early age does not know color or shapes. I   had 20-20 vision up to the age of fifteen, and I am what is known as a blinded person. I know what the color green is, or what white-walled tires look like. In 1938 I lost my sight when streamlined cars were coming in, so I know what they look like. But I have no idea what a jet plane looks like.

When I dream, I am able to picture my sister, but I see her face as I saw it in 1939. A person born blind also dreams, but in words and sensations; he cannot see color or picture it, even in a dream.

Bill also included the following remarks in his address:

> The first time you eat out with a blind person, you might be a bit uneasy as to whether the blind person will spill everything. Often people don't pay attention to their own meals because they are much too concerned with the blind person. If you want to know what to do, just ask him. He'll tell you what he wants. Usually he butters his own bread, puts milk and sugar in his coffee, and cuts his own meat.

> People wonder if they should help a blind person cross the street. Just ask the person, and he will tell you if he needs your help [and how best to do it].

> Some people are under the false impression that blind people are also deaf. One day as I was preparing to cross the street, two elderly ladies nearby noticed me. One lady said to the other, "Let's stand here and see if he can make it." Well, I did.

****

It was while Bill Gallagher was a student at Perkins that he met the extraordinary man who would change his life—Father Thomas J. Carroll, who was chaplain at the school and also taught religion. Father Carroll was popular with the students and spent a great deal of time talking with them about blindness, a subject that would become the focus of his own life's work--improving education and quality of life for blind and blinded persons. He recognized Bill as a young man of great potential, vision, and dedication--a young man who would become his protégé--a young man who might one day do great things for the blind.

Born in Gloucester, Massachusetts in 1909, Father Carroll studied Greek, Latin, and Philosophy at Holy Cross College in Worcester, Massachusetts, graduating in 1932. He was one of eight children in the Carroll family, with seven sisters. Deciding to become a priest, he attended St. John's Seminary, and was ordained in 1938. The Catholic Guild for All the Blind, in the Archdiocese of Boston was organized in 1936. In 1938, Father Carroll became Assistant Director.

Bill remembers meeting Father Carroll during his first year at Perkins. He stated, "I got to know Father Carroll well enough to be comfortable discussing my educational goals and future plans with him. He wanted to know how I felt about going to college, what I wanted to major in, and what school I wanted to attend. He always needled me, saying that there was only one school to attend and that was the College of the Holy Cross in Worcester, his alma mater. I told him that I rooted for the Boston College football team, arch-rivals of Holy Cross!"

When Bill neared graduation, Father Carroll arranged for him to interview with the president of Holy Cross and helped him to present a convincing argument about his abilities, his interest in being active in student government, and his determination to succeed. Father Carroll even pointed out that Bill had been vice president of his class at Perkins (failing to mention that it was a class of only two students!). The Holy Cross administration was so impressed that they offered Bill a four-year scholarship. Bill liked to joke that Father used Bill's sister's transcript to fool the Holy Cross admissions office – whiting out her name and substituting Bill's.

****

The summer before college, Bill spent a great deal of time traveling with Father Carroll. They visited Old Farms Convalescent Hospital School for the War Blinded Service Men in Avon, Connecticut, and Valley Forge Hospital in Phoenixville, Pennsylvania, the hospital at which newly blinded servicemen received medical attention. Both facilities were operated by the Army.

Bill recalled, "By this time, Father Carroll was

gaining national recognition as an authority on blindness. He traveled frequently to Washington and other appropriate places to see what was needed for the war-blinded servicemen. He was especially concerned about rehabilitation for the adventitiously blind person. He wanted to figure out the essential components of a comprehensive rehabilitation program for adventitiously blind persons.

Carroll tried to determine where he could make the most impact on the system. One of the big issues that attracted his enthusiasm was that he might be able to help change the general public's attitude toward blindness while changing the attitude of the blind individual toward the general public. However, if he left Boston, what would happen to those people to whom he could no longer give individual attention? The decision was hard for him; he was so close to many of us on an individual basis. He and I discussed this issue during many of our trips in the car. Eventually, he decided to step onto the national scene, and his influence there was great."

Rocks: The Blind Guy at the Lake

Rocks: The Blind Guy at the Lake

Oh, say what is that thing called light

Which I must never enjoy

What are the blessings of the sight,

Tell your poor blind boy.

Collie Cibber

THE HOLY CROSS COLLEGE YEARS

Perkins prepared the way

For that momentous day

When Rocks would begin

The most important journey

of his life

To prove that he could go it alone

Away from Perkins and

From home

In a sighted community of

Men

Who became his kith

and Kin

Thomas P. Costello

Bill Gallagher entered Holy Cross College as a student in September 1944 and graduated four years later, in June 1948. Bill's roommate for three of his four years at Holy Cross was a veteran named William B. Furlong, also known as Bill, and a member of the class of 1947. He had been blinded on a battlefield in Normandy only a few months before arriving at Holy Cross, and although he regained a significant degree of his vision over time, he and Bill Gallagher clearly had a good deal in common. As Bill Furlong's son Tom put it: "Holy Cross had the foresight to pair Gallagher with Furlong. The two men happened to share an upbeat outlook on life, a blend of idealism and realism leavened by a good-natured sense of humor." One winter night, a group of students that included both Bills made their way into a department store window in Worcester, where they relaxed in a living room set, uncorked a bottle of Champagne, and toasted passersby.

It was Bill Furlong who gave Bill Gallagher a nickname that would last the rest of his life: "Rocks." One day in the dining hall at Holy Cross, Furlong caught Gallagher stuffing rolls into his pockets after dinner. He immediately confronted Gallagher about his theft and said: "Right now I'm reading a book about a petty thief like yourself. His name is Rocks, so from this day forward, I dub you 'Rocks.'"

And so it was that Rocks carried that moniker to his grave, and proudly so.

When Bill Furlong was a senior and about to graduate, he approached a classmate of Bill Gallagher's named Richard O'Keefe and told him he was the right person to be Gallagher's roommate for the last year of college. Furlong said that a group of other students agreed with him about this. O'Keefe was "honored and delighted. I never hesitated. I accepted right on the spot." O'Keefe remembered: "Rocks was very easy to live with and never made demands. In fact, he would go out of his way to be considerate of others. We did not cater to him, and he returned the compliment [by never asking for special treatment]. There was never an aura of any shortcoming that Rocks might have. We tried to help set him up for the real world that he would become part of after graduation. We teased him a lot; there were lots of laughs. Each one of us was independent. Gallagher was treated as we might treat any other student. To put it plainly and simply, he was one of the guys." O'Keefe recalls Rocks was a great lover of popular music of the time. He owned more than three hundred swing records and sang "in the loudest and most satisfied monotone that you have ever heard." He had autographs from many stars in his collection, including Bob Eberle (a singer with Jimmy Dorsey's orchestra), Helen O'Connell (who also sang with Dorsey), and Jimmy Dorsey himself.

O'Keefe, the grandson of Irish immigrants, had grown up in

Rocks: The Blind Guy at the Lake

Harrison, New York, and his prowess on his high school's football team earned him a scholarship to Holy Cross. In 1944, after finishing high school, he volunteered for the Army Air Corps as an air cadet and received an honorable discharge in November 1945. He then went directly to Holy Cross, where he played varsity football. Sports were also a passion for Rocks, who loved football, baseball, and basketball. After graduation the two men would go to football games together, and Rocks always had a very good idea of what was going on down on the field.

O'Keefe remembered that even as a student Rocks had one vision in life: to work with the blinded community after graduating from Holy Cross. He spoke often of Father Thomas Carroll and frequently expressed his gratitude for all that Father Carroll had done for him.

David O'Connor, class of 1950, remembers seeing Rocks on the Holy Cross campus many times, walking on his own without any assistance whatsoever—no cane, no seeing-eye dog, no one to assist or lead him. Within the familiar confines of Holy Cross, Bill preferred not to use any assistance. He disliked the idea of using a cane because of the stereotype of a blind person with cane, dark glasses, and tin cup, helpless to make his own way.

David did not meet Rocks until he was introduced to him at a well-known rathskeller (popular student bar) in New York City after a Holy Cross game at Madison Square Garden. There were about fifteen Holy Cross students at a large table enjoying a few glasses of beer and reminiscing about the events of the game. David recalls that he was briefly introduced to Rocks but had no conversation with him at all. Several months later while walking on the campus, David was passing by Rocks and said, "Hi, Rocks." Rocks responded immediately, "Hi, David. How are you?" Needless to say, David was stunned at Rocks's ability to remember his name from the sound of his voice after so much time had elapsed.

Bill's amazing memory and confidence made an impact on a

reporter named Frances Fiset, a well known columnist in the Boston and Worcester area, who wrote an insightful article about him. Fiset marveled, "He knows the exact spot where the roots of a tree have gently raised the sidewalk, right at the place where he must turn left to go from Alumni to O'Kane Hall. Bill's leather heels flash out a regular Morse Code of messages to his listening ears. Wooden floors, cement walks, gravel, tar, grass, and even welcome mats tap out secret directions to familiar places."

Bill's social graces also impressed Ms. Fiset. "Bill was a fine dancer. At the Purple Key Dance last April, he danced every number. The young lady whom he escorted from his home town, Maynard, was said to have been the loveliest at the ball. . . . Bill's popularity with the other students rose steadily as it became generally known that some of the loveliest girls from Clark [University in Worcester, MA] were visiting Porter's Lodge (the lobby of O'Kane Hall) to read to Bill."

****

When Bill was accepted by Holy Cross, he was accepted on one condition – he must have people read to him on a regular basis to cover his class reading assignments. Father Carroll got in touch with Mrs. Joseph K. McKeon, a teacher in the Worcester school system, and sought her advice. Mrs. McKeon approached Dean Little of Clark University and explained that she needed readers on a daily basis to help a student with his class assignments. Retaining his scholarship at Holy Cross depended on it. Could he ask some Clark students to help out? He kindly agreed to the request on the condition that the readers not allow the activity to interfere with their own school work.

Marion McCann was one of the founders of the Newman Club at Clark and its first president. She was recruited to be one of Bill's readers, and she gladly accepted the invitation. Her father, a teacher, was a graduate of Holy Cross, and her brother, a local judge, was as well. According to Marion, there were about thirty young women who volunteered to read for Bill. They would go in pairs to the campus on a rotating basis five afternoons a week from 3 to 5 o'clock, and read for an hour each. They met in a secluded nook in the lobby of O'Kane Hall where the reading could take place in quiet.

Marion recalls that Bill was "very pleasant, a young man of great spirit. He was very meticulous in the manner in which he kept his personal belongings. Everything was in proper order so that he could find exactly what he wanted—a shirt, a comb, a book, shoes, and so on. His classmates in their mischievous ways would rearrange the whole caboodle. You might expect that this would make him mad, but his reaction was the opposite. He enjoyed the fun and games his class played on him. In all probability, this made him feel that he was one of the boys."

The fact that Bill never took notes amazed Marion, as did his ability to determine, when he was standing at a bus stop, whether there was a tree, a lamp post, or a telephone pole nearby. He could even tell which one it was. She could never understand how he was able to do this but vaguely recalls that it had something to do with a change in air pressure.

Bill Gallagher had one date with Marion, a formal affair probably sponsored by the naval ROTC at Holy Cross. The men at the dance told Marion how pretty she looked, and she was happy to find that Bill was a wonderful dancer. She remembers that at the Clark senior prom, Bill "was the most popular guy at the dance" and that all of her friends wanted to dance with him.

Another reader, Virginia Carroll Hedberg, remembers that senior prom at Clark, because a number of Bill's readers had convinced him to attend the prom with one of the seniors, also a reader, who didn't have a date. "So the blind man had a blind date," Virginia says. She also remembers that he was a great dancer, but that his partners had to help direct him in order to avoid bumping into other dancing couples. She also recalls that at some of the reading sessions, Bill would often interrupt the readers because he wanted to talk rather than listen to his lesson. The girls would protest: "We have to read to you." "Are you getting paid for this?" he would ask them, and they would answer "no." "Then why worry about it?" he would say, and they never had an answer to that.

Bill himself remembered that his roommate Bill Furlong became somewhat envious of the female attention he was receiving. "Once, he put on some sunglasses and pretended to be me for one reading session. Someone came in and asked him if he was Bill Gallagher and he nodded yes. "Good," the voice said. "I'm Mary Sullivan's father. She couldn't make it today so I'm reading in her place. Poor Furlong had to sit there and listen to this guy read for over an hour!"

When both colleges were on vacation, several Worcester teachers and other residents carried on the pleasant task of reading to Bill. These included Margaret M. Walsh and Matthew J. Coriming of the Classical High faculty, William V. Callan of Grafton Street Junior High, Ms. Mary Mulhane and Mrs. Joseph McKeon of Ledge Street School, Mrs. Redican, and Mrs. Florence Driscoll, a former teacher.

****

All of Rock's friends have stories about the incredible skill with which Rocks memorized the terrain, the buildings, trees and shrubs on the Holy Cross campus, and how he could navigate them unerring, even when walking alone. Tom Costello's favorite story was about a rainy day, when a group of students were looking out the window of a room on first Carlin, and spotted Rocks coming out of Kimball. Just before the steps entering Carlin was a deep indentation, worn there by thousands of students' feet, tramping in and out of the building down the years. On this day, it was full of a deep puddle of rainwater. Rog DesRoches said, "Watch the little bugger, he'll walk right around it," which, of course, was just what Rocks did, stepping carefully around the puddle and up the steps, just as though he could see it. He did not have to see the puddle; he just knew it was there.

Another favorite incident occurred when Rocks and a

couple of other classmates stayed at John Becker's house in Walpole on a Saturday night, when a snowstorm left a foot of snow in the driveway. Tom Costello recalls, "When we all went out to shovel in the morning, to my amazement, Rocks insisted on going out with us. I put a shovel in his hand, had him touch the top of the snow pile and he went right at it with the rest of us. Rocks didn't want to be left out of things. Clearly, he did not allow his sightlessness to leave him out of life."

Part of the magic of Rocks was his acquired ability to look a person dead in the eye to such an extent that innumerable people failed to be able to recognize him as a blinded person.

****

Senior year, Tom Costello was running for the office of President of the Senior Class. He remembers, "The pre-election period was an exciting time on the campus, with each candidate having his own election committee. Posters and signs and throw-aways were everywhere. Rocks was my chief opponent." Unquestionably, and rightfully so, Costello recalls, Rocks was the most popular man on campus.

A few days before the election, Costello's roommate Bill Loftus asked him, "How come you are not doing any campaigning?" Tom responded, "Well, Bill, everyone in our class knows me. If they want me as their President, they will vote for me."

Bill asked Tom if he had any objection to him and Ray Carey forming a campaign committee to promote his candidacy. Tom replied, "None whatsoever."

The morning of the election arrived. Tom was astounded when he went into the common bathroom, used by all the students on that floor, and discovered a large poster which read, "Vote for Costello For President" on every mirror and over every sink. The same large poster was found over every urinal and in every bathroom stall in every senior bathroom on campus. As this blitz of posters occurred on the morning of election day, it gave no chance to Gallagher's Committee to counter the Loftus-Carey strategy. Costello won the election hands down.

To this day, Costello recalls, there are members of the class who were Rocks' supporters, who look at him with some resentment because of the great upset engineered by Carey, Loftus & Co. "I can't blame them for feeling that way," he comments. "Rocks was so beloved."

****

THE CHAMPIONSHIP BASKETBALL SEASON

Memories of the years Bill attended Holy Cross would not be complete without mention of the championship basketball season. On March 25, 1947, the Holy Cross basketball team accomplished what no other basketball team from New England ever had by beating the University of Oklahoma at Madison Square Garden and winning the NCAA (National Collegiate Athletic Association) Division 1 championship tournament. The Holy Cross Crusaders had no senior on the team and not even a home court, but they had great spirit and the will to win. Although the teamwork and the individual performances were superb, many give much of the credit to Bill Gallagher, who was present at every game, sitting on the bench and giving encouragement and inspiration to each player.

Bill himself described his involvement with the players at a pre-game dinner in March of that season: "I have seen every game this season, through play-by-play announcers beside me, players who knew everyone on both teams and knew what, how, and why individuals and teams were doing on the court... The crowd noises, the reactions on the bench, the gaps in cheering tell me how the game is progressing. When someone tells me that Haggerty or Mullaney just hooked in a basket and then I hear the players rushing back in defense, I hope that the other team will miss. I know that when I go to the NCAA tournament that our team has the spirit and the ability to do well."

Sports writer Vern Miller described sitting on the Holy Cross bench next to Rocks for the NCAA game against Navy, which Holy Cross won at Madison Square Garden.

"The team worships Billy. Before they entered the game, each player wrung his hand. Tears glistened in Gallagher's perfect blue eyes so straightforward that few people realize that they catch no light. Before the game Rocks was nervous. He fingered his Braille watch for the time. He spoke excitedly, "The time has come for my boys to win." . . . The game began and Bill's ability to follow play was almost eerie. His head moved up and down the court with the ball. He could tell when the ball was being shot and when it struck the backboard. Holy Cross dropped behind at the outset of play, nine points in all. Gallagher was not despondent. His face was red from shouting and he had broken out into a cold sweat. He kept a perfect tabulation of the score.

Then Joe Mullaney and George Kaftan sparked the team up to Navy's score. Gallagher jumped with joy, his entire fragile frame pulsating with responsive energy. A photographer snapped a picture. The flash bulb exploded its momentary burst of light. "You see that light? I can always catch the impulse of a photographer's flash." [Gallagher liked to joke with photographers by saying "Watch it with those flashbulbs. You could blind a guy."] Half time score was 29-27 in favor of Holy Cross. The Worcester radio station wanted Gallagher to speak over the radio. I volunteered to take him up to the gallery broadcasting booth. Bill just barely held the back of my arm as I plunged through the swirling masses. Never have I led interference so proudly. It was unbelievable how agilely Bill followed. He could detect my reaching for a stair and climbed easily without being told that there were steps. He followed in and out up four flights of stairs, and I doubt whether one person we passed knew that he was blind.

Rocks: The Blind Guy at the Lake

Bill spoke over the radio, spoke in excited gasps as any lad whose team is winning might spill over. I remember he started saying: "The way I see this game is ..." Following the interview, we worked our way through the mob in double-quick time. Holy Cross fans were everywhere. They all hailed Bill, who is one of the most popular boys around Pakachoag Hill. Chuck Graver described the second half vividly for Bill. As Holy Cross drew ahead with a comfortable though not a commanding lead, Gallagher's brimful bowl of happiness increased. He jumped to his feet with mighty cheers after every basket.

When the game ended, a swirl of happy players dragged Bill Gallagher to the dressing room. He stood there pumping hands and reminding each player of the errors he had made and the beautiful shots he had connected. ... Now I know that nowhere was Holy Cross's victory so splendid and magnificent as in the sightless eyes of courageous Bill Gallagher. And no basketball team has ever had a mascot who meant more to the players."

Rocks told a reporter for the Worcester *Telegram and Gazette* how it came about that he was permitted to sit on the Holy Cross bench. "I sat next to Ken Haggerty in philosophy class. He was the basketball co-captain. He asked me if I'd like to go to a game and maybe he could talk the coach, Doggie Julian, into letting me sit on the bench." The coach agreed and Bill went to the Holy Cross game against Manhattan on January 21, 1947, at Boston Garden. After the game, Julian, a superstitious sort who would rub his player's foreheads in the huddle for good luck, invited Bill along for the rest of the ride. Some called him the team's mascot; others called him the Crusaders' good luck charm.

Charley Graver was a substitute player who most often narrated the progress of the game for Rocks. As Graver tells it, "Rocks was down at the end of the bench, and I didn't get a lot of playing time. That's when the good Lord asked me: "Why don't you go down and be his eyes?' That's how it all began. . . . Rocks would jump up and cheer while the shot was still in the air, somehow knowing it was going in. He had an unbelievable sixth sense." Victory after victory, Graver sat alongside Rocks and did a running play-by-play account of the action: "And now Joe [Mullaney] passes over to Dermie [O'Connell], who feeds the fall into the pivot to George [Kaftan]."

Bill later recounted: "Charley did a fantastic job on the play by play. Of course, being a player, he knew how the plays were designed and where every pass was going before it was made. When he got into a game, another teammate would slide over and take his place as my private announcer."

With Bill Gallagher sitting on the bench, the Holy Cross Crusaders won nineteen games in a row, including the NCAA tournament victories over Navy, City College of New York, and the final championship game over Oklahoma before 18,445 fans. The Crusaders exulted at mid-court, hugging their trophy and each other. Right in the middle of the big squeeze was Rocks Gallagher.

Bill himself had this to say about his participation in the team effort. "In life you don't look up at people and you don't look down on people. You meet everyone at the same level and look them square in the eyes. That's what these guys from Holy Cross did. They met me on an individual level, treated me as part of the team, and didn't put me of in a corner somewhere. That is called character, and that's why these men will always be champions."

****

CINDERELLA, 50 YEARS LATER

"The 50th Reunion of the Holy Cross 1947 NCAA Basketball Champions last Saturday (February 22, 1997) was a once in a lifetime emotional experience," wrote John Becker, Class Agent for the Class of '48. "I have been involved in practically every imaginable kind of event at Holy Cross over the years and none of them even comes close in its effect on this old grad. The same feelings were expressed by all of the 1947 players and members of the Class of '48, who were there. The most important of them was Rocks Gallagher.

Rocks: The Blind Guy at the Lake

"Rocks drew on his seemingly limitless reserve of courage, inner toughness, resiliency and resolve to make the difficult trip from Webster, Massachusetts, to the Hart Center at Holy Cross for the reunion ceremonies." He was a very sick man at the time.

John wrote about the reunion from his perspective:

"All the old players, widows and Rocks lined up at center court to a tremendous ovation from the capacity crowd while the band played the alma mater. Many of them were teary eyed.

It is interesting to note that both Rocks and Charlie Graver sat side by side at center court, both in wheelchairs. These same two men had sat side by side on the bench all through the championship season = sans wheelchairs."

John Becker remembers that Rocks made the huge effort with the help of Frank Marshall and others, including the recently deceased Joe Mullaney, to come up to the Cross and participate in the 50th Reunion of the 1947 basketball champions. The most riveting memory of that event was the meeting of Rocks and Chuck Graver, old and dear friends, for the first time in 50 years, both in wheelchairs. Tearfully, they entwined one another's hands and forearms, the closest they could come to a warm embrace. It was an emotional moment for all that were there and seemed it would go on forever. At this point, Mullaney tapped them both on the head and said, "Okay, break it up you guys. We're going to have a wheelchair race to see who can get out to mid court first." Only Joe could think of something like that and get away with actually saying it. The remark cracked up all of us there and we went on to the festivities.

Several excellent accounts in the newspapers at the time of the Reunion gave a birds eye view of the miraculous happenings of the champion season of 1946-1947. John Gearan, Holy Cross Class of '65, wrote one of these accounts for the Sunday Telegram (Worcester):

Rocks: The Blind Guy at the Lake

HC FANS CHEER 1947 NATIONAL CHAMPS

They accomplished what no other Division 1 basketball team from New England ever has. In 1947 Holy Cross was crowned NCAA champ in Madison Square Garden. A team without a senior and without a home court won it all.

Yesterday, a near capacity crowd at the Hart Center cheered that golden team on the occasion of the 50th Anniversary of its monumental victory.

As they were called to midcourt, Crusader fans applauded long, loud and respectfully. Bob Cousy, who went on to become "Mr. Basketball." George Kaftan, the NCAA Tournament's MVP. Andy Laska, who became Assumption College's most illustrious coach. Joe Mullaney, the innovative Providence College coach who later coached the pros. His brother Dave Mullaney, a JV player that year. Charlie Bollinger, the "Big Man" in the middle. Jim Riley, Charlie Graver, rolling out in a wheelchair pushed by his wife Mae and throwing a fist into the air to the delight of the gathering. Co-captain Ken Haggerty. And the team's good luck charm, Bill "Rocks" Gallagher, who sat on the bench as a blind HC student during the ride to the championship.

Representing the deceased members of that famed team were Frank Oftring, Jr., whose dad went on to coach Holy Cross; Jay Curran, there for his dad Bob, a Worcester guy who became head coach at UMass, head baseball coach at Holy Cross and HC Hoop Assistant; Mrs. Alvin Julian, the widow of coach Doggie Julian; Helen O'Connell, wife of the late Dermie O'Connell; and Mrs. Bob McMullan.

The ceremony was touching and classy in its simplicity and tears of nostalgia filled many eyes. At a commemorative banquet highlighted by films of the championship game while toastmaster Rowe, a Worcester guy who coached UConn in the '70's, delighted the crowd.

'I hope fans never forget how great this team was. It wasn't how they won it all. They had great players and played in a style way above their era much like Michael Jordan does today,' said Toby Julian, the coach's son who starred at Classical and later played for his dad at Dartmouth."

Gearan also wrote a column for the Telegram entitled:

"HC's LUCKY CHARM – MAGIC TWOSOME INSPIRED PURPLE"

They had not sat next to each other along a basketball sideline in 50 years. But yesterday there they were. Charlie Graver and "Rocks" Gallagher, at a Holy Cross game together. Just like old times, except now they were confined to wheelchairs.

They are fighting tough illness these days and made monumental efforts to return to campus to be with their 1947 NCAA championship team.

Back then Graver and Gallagher were special teammates, both sitting in the very end of the Holy Cross bench.

Graver a 27 year old freshman and World War II veteran, had been *tossed a basketball scholarship by Crusader coach "Doggie" Julian.*

William 'Rocks' Gallagher had earned an academic scholarship after graduating from the Perkins School for the Blind.

Rocks: The Blind Guy at the Lake

I sat next to Ken Haggerty in Philosophy class. Ken was the basketball co-captain, recalled Gallagher. He asked me if I'd like to go to a game and maybe he could talk Doggie into letting me sit on the bench.

"It was a different world back then. There were no big-time sneaker contracts; TV money or March Madness. Coach Julian saw nothing wrong with letting a blind student sit on his bench. He was a nice man, Doggie Julian. So Haggerty brought Gallagher to the Manhattan game in the Boston Garden, where Holy Cross played six "home" games that season, and arranged to have Rocks sit on the bench. The Crusaders practiced in a campus barn and had no court of their own.

"So Gallagher sat and listened and felt the excitement of the game on that January 21, 1947. He had been an athlete at Maynard High before going blind when his optic nerves went on the fritz, so he could sense what was happening. Holy Cross beat Manhattan and Julian, a superstitious sort who would rub his player's foreheads in the huddle for good luck, invited Gallagher along for the rest of the ride. Some called Gallagher, endearingly, the team's mascot and others Holy Cross's good luck charm.

"Rocks was down at the end of the bench and I didn't get a lot of playing time," explained Graver. "That's when the Good Lord asked me, "Why don't you go down and be his eyes." That's how it began.

"Victory upon victory, Graver sat alongside Gallagher and did a running play-by-play account of the game action. "And now Joe (Mullaney) passes over to Dermie (O'Connell) who feeds the ball into the pivot to George (Kaftan)." Graver would rat-a-tat as Gallagher would hang on every phrase and visualize every play.

"Rocks would jump up and cheer while the shot was still in the air, somehow knowing it was going in. He had an unbelievable sixth sense," said Graver.

"Charlie did a fantastic job on the play-by-play. Of course, being a player he knew how the plays were designed and where every pass was going before it was made," said Gallagher. "When Charlie got into a game, another teammate would slide over and take his place as my private announcer."

"With Gallagher as their good luck charm, Holy Cross won 19 in a row, including NCAA tournament victories over Navy, City College of New York and finally, in March 25, 1947, over Oklahoma. The Crusaders exulted at mid-court in Madison Square Garden before 18,445 fans, hugging their trophy and each other. Right in the middle of the big squeeze was Rocks Gallagher.

"Yesterday, you could see a glimmer of love in the eyes of the eight surviving champs as they watched Rocks Gallagher, once again, embrace that championship trophy on the court at the Hart Center.

"Gallagher had shown remarkable courage in a much different way. An avid athlete who went blind rose up from adversity to graduate from high school and the Perkins School, earning a scholarship to Holy Cross. At the college on the hill, Gallagher never used a cane or a seeing-eye dog. He counted each of the hundreds of steep steps and negotiated his way without physical help from class to class.

After that glorious season, Graver and Gallagher parted ways.

Graver, who came from a coal mining town of Summit Hill, Pennsylvania, had worked after high school and fought in the war. "A Jewish guy who knew Doggie recruited me. I was 27 and just out of the service. I got a telegram from Doggie which simply said he had a scholarship and an open spot for me. I was born a Lutheran, but I didn't hesitate at Doggie's offer," explained Graver, 77 and a retired executive of a national food enterprise.

****

How important was Rocks Gallagher to the success of the NCAA Championship team? For those who doubt the truth of the legend that Rocks was a decisive factor in that winning season, we turn to two of the most famous players on that team – Bob Cousy and George Kaftan- for their insight on the part played by Gallagher.

The Holy Cross Magazine, spring edition 2000, had an article entitled, "Holy Cross Athletics Timeline," which reviewed all of the accomplishments of the great athletes who attended the College from 1843 to the present.

A special committee, made up of Dave Anderson, '51, Bob Gamere, '62, Maureen Milliken, '83 and Dan Shaughnessy, was appointed to determine the top ten Holy Cross athletes of all time. The following were rated 2 to 10 :

2.	Tom Heinsohn	'56	Basketball
2.	Dr. William T. Osmanski	'39	Football and Head Coach
2.	Louis F. Sockalexis	'97	Baseball
2.	Tie Ronald S. Perry	'54	Basketball
2.	Tie Ronald K. Perry	'80	Basketball
2.	Jon N. Morris	'64	Football
2.	Tie Togo Palazzi	'54	Basketball
2.	Tie Gordie Lockbaum	'88	Football
2.	Tie Albert "Hop" Riopel	'24	Coach and Football Player
2.	Tie John s. Provost	'75	Football

Bob Cousy, '50, was rated the number one Holy Cross athlete of all time.

The selection committee wrote of Bob Cousy: "Mr. Basketball," "The Houdini of the Hardwood," "The Cooz" – call him what you will, Bob Cousy has single-handedly changed the way basketball is played today. A broken right arm at the age of 13 forced him to learn to dribble and shoot with his left. This ambidexterity led to the famous behind-the-back dribble. Although not the creator of this move, he did help to popularize it while at Holy Cross.

"He earned the All-American title four consecutive years at Holy Cross and became one of the biggest names in college hoops. In his senior year, the crusaders won 26 straight games and finished second in the National Invitational Tournament."

"Cousy's acquisition in 1950, proved to be a lucky break for the Celtics, who ended their season with a winning record. In his third year as an NBA player, Cousy began to establish his legend. His expertise as a point guard drove and inspired the team. His sharp peripheral vision and amazing dribbling skills kept the ball away from defenders long enough for his team-mates to develop successful plays. Cousy played a key role in the Celtics operation, as they dominated the basketball scene from 1959 through 1966. Cousy played in 13 NBA All-Star games, where he earned the MVP title twice. He has been inducted into the Basketball Hall of Fame and named to the NBA's 25th, 35th and 50th Anniversary Teams. In 1974, an Associated Press poll selected him one of the top five basketball players of all time. Recently, the "Boston Globe" chose the top 100 athletes of the Twentieth Century and ranked Cousy number eight."

Dave Anderson, '51, Pulitzer Prize winning journalist and for over fifty years one of the truly great sports writers in our nation, wrote in the "Holy Cross Magazine" "Of all the Holy Cross athletes, Bob Cousy is not only head and shoulders above the others, but legs and sneakers above. No other Holy Cross athlete has provided the impact on his sport that Cooz did, not only at the Cross, but also with the Celtics, in so many of their NBA championship seasons. The College has never had another like him, and may never in the future have another like him."

In assessing the importance of Rocks Gallagher to the

Rocks: The Blind Guy at the Lake

NCAA Championship Team of 1947, Bob Cousy wrote in 2003:

> *The NCAA was not the big deal it is today, however, it is safe to say that Holy Cross winning in 1947 is probably the most unlikely champion they've ever had and the most compelling in that, that sport had just been resumed at Holy Cross. We practiced in a barn and Doggie (Julian) did not recruit. So how the hell did we do it? In my humble opinion it had a lot to do with 'chemistry.'*

> *Rocks directly played a major role in creating the chemistry that complimented our talent and motivated and goosed our natural high competitive instincts. It is not subjective but so often it is captured it makes such a difference in competition at every level (team competition) where opponents are fairly evenly matched. It certainly did in our case even though we might not have realized it at the time. It was a 'magical moment' and Rocks deserves a large part of the credit. He was daily living proof to a group of impressionable young jocks how determination, will power, etc., could overcome adversity. He was just the inspiration that a talented group of "under-dogs" needed and we rode it to the championship. '*

In 1984, Rocks was nominated to receive an Honorary Degree by the College of Holy Cross. In seconding that nomination, Cousy wrote the following letter in 1985 to Reverand John E. Brooks, SJ, the President of the College:.

> *Those of us who were at Holy Cross with "Rocks" remember well his display of courage and indomitable spirit in dealing with his affliction then, at a young age. Since then, he has been a continual*

inspirational source as he commits his life to persons without sight while he almost literally conducts his life and affairs as if 'sighted.'

The manner in which he has 'carried his cross' in life and in fact turned it into a positive instrument to help others personifies, in my opinion, the Catholic values that Holy Cross has always tried to instill in its students and deserved acknowledgment.

For his own part, Rocks stated, "I never could forget 'Cous' for all the time he gave me during that year in school and in years to follow. Cous and I were roomies and on road trips I'll always remember him for what he did following the Holy Cross win over Oklahoma for the NCAA Championship in 1947.

Cousy was the hero of that game and was being mobbed by his teammates on the floor, as someone told me at the time. But he rushed over to where I was still sitting on the bench to give me a full report on what transpired, describing the immediate celebration of the Holy Cross players and rooters. Although he was the big man of the game, 'Cous' found time for me.

Cous' job as my reporter did not end with our college days. I often 'saw' him play as a pro with the Celtics, and after the games, we would get together and he would tell me what went right or wrong in the games, and would give me a personal rundown on the other players."

****

In the championship season of '47, when Holy Cross won the National Basketball Crown, George Kaftan was chosen as the MVP of the NCAA Tournament held at Madison Square Garden. He was also selected as the first All American in basketball from the College. One of his great accomplishments was becoming the first Holy Cross player to score more than 1,000 points in a season. After George graduated from Holy Cross in 1949, he had a successful basketball career starting with the Boston Celtics, for whom he played from 1949 to 1951. He then played for the New York Knicks in 1952 and 1953, and ended his pro career with the Bullets in 1954.

George remembers:

Rocks was an integral part of our team. Where we went, he went. Where we ate, he ate. Where we partied, he partied and I might say, he was the favorite of the crowd. And when it came to game time, Rocks always had his seat at the end of the bench. He had the uncanny ability to know who had the ball and who was running up and down the court. He could recognize the players by the distinctive sound each one of us made as our sneakers pounded the hardwood and every once in a while, I would hear his voice as I raced by the bench, 'Go, Greek, go.'

****

With America at war abroad on two fronts, the challenges that faced members of the class of 1948 were great. Andrew McNearney, one of Rocks's classmates, wrote a history of the class of 1948 for the senior class Year Book, giving a vivid picture of life at Holy Cross in those momentous days:

The history of the Class of Nineteen Hundred and Forty-Eight can be summed up simply as a "Return to Normalcy." That precisely has been our objective, our goal and our whole concentrated effort ever since that memorable day in the late Summer of '45, when the great tide of insecurity and uncertainty began to roll back from the Hill and we began to grasp the full significance of the celebrations, and could first say, and finally believe our voices, "The War is OVER!!"

This common goal has been one of the most powerful forces in uniting the Class. There is no doubt that we have become one of the most compact units in the recent history of Alma Mater, but we were not always so. We come from many [social] classes and all walks of life. We are nineteen years old and we are twenty-nine. We came here as early as September, 1937 and as late as September, 1947. [ii]We were on the Hill as civilians and Navy students during the War; we are both civilians and Navy students today. But above all we have become men of Holy Cross. . . . the Class of '48.

We represent a decade on Mount St. James. Holy Cross College is built on land that is called Mount St. James. The College is built on a small mountain that rises from its lowest point from a river to a peak that gives one a wondrous view of the City of Worcester. Our professors have witnessed a temporary halt in the "passing parade, while the same men they saw as long as ten years ago are still answering to their names in the classroom and greeting them on the paths of the campus.

In the late '30's, as today, we were welcomed as Freshmen by the Keymen[iii], who showed us the marvels of the campus. Father Leo Shea met us and when he appointed a grievance committee, we marveled at student democracy.

We watched-- fascinated-- while Ronny Cahill, Hank Oulette, Bill Osmanski, Giardi, Kelley, Turner and Company performed their[football] magic on Fitton Field under the able direction of Coach Anderson. And we saw the marvels of Coach Barry's nine as they held up the reputation of the College in baseball – which was no mean task, since for longer than anyone can remember we have been at the very top in collegiate baseball, the ones to beat.

*The ominous rumblings on the far distant shores of Asia and Europe were becoming louder, but we were too busy with Father Brennan's tremendous English assignments and Father Dwyer's four hundred lines a night of "Tacitus to pay too much attention. A few of us were drafted, and we thought it was a big joke that would just blow over. But the rumbling grew . . . and grew . . . and then it was upon us . . . **WAR!!***

Rocks: The Blind Guy at the Lake

War came to Holy Cross. Each day there were more official envelopes [draft notices] in the P.O. Boxes; each day another few left. There was little drama connected with these departures. A last Coke in the café, a last round of hand shakes, and then another empty bed in Alumni or Carlin, another missing man at meals. Gradually, we got accustomed to the sudden disappearance of a friend or acquaintance, until outwardly there was no more attention given to their departures than "What happened to him . . .?" and the simple reply, "Uncle Sam."

At last there grew up many groups that were outwardly different on this campus that had long been noted for its solidarity and unity. Among the Navy Units, there were those who loved the College as have all the "Cross Men" in the past,and there were those who cared very little for Holy Cross. Among the civilians there were those who had been rejected by the military services, those who were not yet old enough to go, and those few who had seen action and were given medical discharges. But these groups, so outwardly different, supplied a number of talented men who fused together in a tightly knit unit and kept intact the traditions which have been synonymous with Holy Cross since 1843.

Classes were running the year 'round. Twelve grueling, exhausting months of teaching, studying, uncertainty. . . and more of the same. Countless conversations began with "Now, before the war. . . " or "After the war, we'll . . ." That was one of the few bright spots that any of us could see. Faculty and students alike looked forward with eager expectancy to the time when Holy Cross would have "returned to normal." It became the goal and constant wish of all of us here on the Hill that all the traditions and customs should be resumed, and should take up their rightful places in our student life--such as the Philosophy Orals, the Logic Specimen, the Freshman athletic teams, the Intramural Leagues, our top-flight Dramatic Society, the Aquinas Circle , Le Croise, and many, many other institutions that were an integral part of Holy Cross . . . before the War.

And then just as the strain was becoming almost

unbearable, just as we were becoming numb from constant study, suddenly, as swiftly as the war had come upon us, there came the Atomic Bomb and the quick capitulation of Japan. . . .and Peace.

We could not comprehend at first all that the coming of peace meant. Most of us who were here at that time did not remember anything but the Holy Cross of wartime. But the Fathers had promised great things for Alma Mater "After the War," and had imbued us with such a fervent desire for the return to the Crusader traditions of old, that we expected a complete change almost immediately.

We were, perhaps, too eager for instant changes, and as the months rolled on we became impatient of delays. With headlong energy we rushed in and set up the societies and restored the traditions that had been abandoned during the War. But the change to peacetime was destined to come more slowly. It would not be rushed. In the Fall of '45 we returned to the status of one of the great football teams as we sent Koslowski, Kissel, Byers, Conroy, Strojny and Company to the Orange Bowl. Several months later, the Dramatic Society returned to pre-war standards with its performance of "A Bell for Adano."

In the Fall of '46, with the advent of the first peacetime scholastic calendar in over five years, the Logic Specimen was resumed, and the Aquinas Circle again took up the pursuit of philosophical questions.

We formed a committee around our classmate Ray Ball and chose a new style of school ring for the Class. That Spring the Junior Prom was revived and was an overwhelming success, everyone agreeing that it was the best social function sponsored on the Hill in years. The Junior Class Committee was elected just before Christmas with Bill Connell acting as Chairman, ably supported by John Linehan, John DiGangi, Joe McCarthy, and John Whalen. They made possible a truly banner year for the Class.

One of the greatest reasons for the success of the

penultimate year was the setting up of machinery to establish the Student Government here on the campus. This was an entirely new activity; we had never before had on organization officially representing the entire student body. Shortly after classes began in the Fall of '47, the Constitution was ratified and the officers of the first Student Congress of the College of the Holy Cross were elected. Bill Connell was chosen the First President after a hard-fought, "dog-eat-dog" campaign, which found Ray Carey and George Guerinot nosed out at the polls.

For the first time in years, the tradition of regular offices for the Senior Class was resumed. We sent Tom Costello into the Presidency by an overwhelming majority, while Bill Gallagher won the First Vice-President's post handily. Second Vice-President, Secretary, and Treasurer, were Hillary Carroll, Ray Ball and John Mahoney. In February, '48, Carroll and Ball graduated and their posts were capably filled by Bob Curran and Bob Mulcahy.

This year, we had the greatest football team since the '45 Orange Bowl squad. Bobby Sullivan at the halfback slot proved one of the finest players seen on Fitton Field in memory. He was the unanimous choice to win the O'Melia trophy for the B. C. (Boston College, another strong football team and arch-rivals of Holy Cross) *game, and easily walked off with the Bulger-Lowe award as the best player in New England. He capped this highly effective season by representing us in the East-West Game, where he all but stole the show.*

Another institution was set up this year when the Senior Class gave the first annual Student-Faculty Smoker to cement more firmly the bond that has always existed between the students and their professors on Mount St. James. This smoker was such a tremendous success that already another has been planned for next year and the consensus is that it will become a tradition. The outstanding contributors to an extremely pleasant evening were Ray Carey, "Monk" Daly, Bill Webster, Gene DeFilippo, John T. Murphy and Tom Costello. Ted O'Rourke was the toastmaster of the affair and the chairmen were Don Gross for the tickets, and

Rocks: The Blind Guy at the Lake

Jack Kickham for entertainment.

In the course of the few short years since the end of the war and the return of peace to the Hill, we have made great strides towards that objective which was held up to us by the faculty – to make our campus as it was and should continue to be in the future. But we have not reached the end of that road. It is true that all the institutions for which we have striven have been set up or revived, but that is only half of the job. They must be kept working smoothly until they have again become the integral part of life here on the Hill that they once were.

We have effected the "return to normalcy" insofar as it was in our power to do so. We have done this as Crusaders, as men of Holy Cross and the Class of 1948. Our work is not without flaws since it is as yet incomplete. The rest of the job rests with those who will take up where we left off.

The Class of 1948 hands down a torch of accomplishment to its successors, to be kept burning brightly . . .pro Dei, pro Patria, pro Sancta Cruse. (For God, for our Country, and for the Holy Cross) (R. Andrew McNearney, '48).

Rocks: The Blind Guy at the Lake

THE BOSTON YEARS

Following his graduation from Holy Cross, Father Carroll assisted Bill in obtaining a two year scholarship to Boston College to study social work, graduating with a Master's Degree in Social Work. Bill recalls that just before starting graduate school, he got "cold feet" and Father Carroll came to his rescue:

We took a few long rides that summer and made some practical plans about where I would live and how I would function independently in the City of Boston. Mobility was a problem; I still had not given in to the cane or the dog. Temporary arrangements were made for me to live with Father Carroll's sister and brother-in-law, who happened to be a psychiatrist. I used sighted guides to go from my living quarters to the school until I made friends with a classmate and we rented a place of our own.

The years at Boston College were a real growing-up period for me, a turning point. Was I going to function independently, or should I look for a program that would shelter me and make me more dependent? Throughout this period, I received precounseling from Father Carroll. However, in the first semester, I didn't do well in my exams. I was just too preoccupied. Going into the exams in the second semester, I was uncomfortable again and quite depressed and didn't think I would do well. I felt like quitting.

One night before an exam, I called Father Carroll. He said that he had a meeting but it would be over by 10:00, and he would pick me up and we'd take a drive. He also said, 'Don't study. Don't open a book.' We rode until 3:00 in the morning; we took Route 9 to the New York State line, turned around, came back, and went up to New Hampshire and back. At 3:00 a.m. he dropped me off where I was living. I slept for a few hours, took the three-hour exam at 8:00 a.m., and knocked off the highest grade that I had ever received in graduate school. The night ride must have helped.

[From "Blindness Rehabilitation in Honor of Thomas J. Carroll: A Festschrift" (a volume of writings by different authors presented as a tribute or memorial, especially to a scholar)

As graduation neared, Bill informed Father Carroll he had decided to take a job with the Commission for the Blind. Father Carroll instead suggested that he find a job in a generic program and then, after that experience, decide in a more objective way whether he wanted to come into the field of blindness. Bill states that he disagreed with Father Carroll but followed his advice, eventually landing a job in Child Welfare for the City of Boston working with dependent and neglected children. Bill remembers, "It was a great experience, and I received good supervision. I also gained confidence. After working with neglected children for five years, I received a call from Father Carroll." During the past five years that Bill was working for the City of Boston, Father Carroll had become Director of the Catholic Guild for the Blind. In 1952 he had brought the idea of safe cane travel skills to the Center in the form of the first mobility program in the world. The following year he conducted the first National Mobility Institute to link the war blind and civilian program of orientation and mobility. In 1954, he established St. Paul's Rehabilitation Center for the Blind, a service of the Catholic Guild for All the Blind. He asked Bill to join the staff as a social worker.

Bill's acceptance of Father Carroll's offer marked the beginning of a new relationship between the two men-- no longer mentor and mentee – but as professionals and colleagues. Bill said of Father Carroll, "He was one of the greatest men working for the blind." He quoted Father Carroll as saying, "A person who loses his sight steps from a bright world into a black world, but in time, finds it changes to gray."

Rachel Rosenbaum, the current Executive Director of the Carroll Center, remembers:

Father had begun this rehabilitation program with little more than good will and a promise of funding from the federal government – in fact, he became involved with the development of writing legislation that would enable Massachusetts to accept federal funds for the Vocational Rehabilitation program, a system still in place a half a century later.

The first years at St. Paul's were heady exciting years as Father with his small band of dedicated staff challenged the beliefs of society about blind persons, a belief first formed at the veteran's Program with WW II vets that emphasized an active participation in life. Father appeared on the newly emerging media; television and was interviewed by prominent journalists; and had several opportunities to discuss his ideas with the public on radio. For Bill it was being at the cutting edge, even if – as he later said – we were paid in Holy water and blessing, but very low salaries even for that day. When Father had to face city inspectors for the somewhat hastily and badly renovated stable which he was using as a classroom, recreation area and dorm, he cleverly delegated Bill to show the inspectors around. According to Bill, Father knew the inspectors would be so awed that a totally blind person had a Masters Degree in social work and was independently walking them through the maze of small staircases and corridors that they would overlook the multiple small infractions of the building code.

Bill was the only blind member of the staff. He interviewed prospective enrollees and after they got to the Center he helped the trainees with individual problems. He also had a heavy schedule of speaking engagements throughout Massachusetts. It was estimated that in performing his duties at the Center, he traveled approximately 15,000 miles each year.

****

Fred Silver first came to know Bill Gallagher in the early 1950s, when both were employed at the Catholic Guild for the Blind in Boston, Massachusetts. When St. Paul's Rehabilitation was opened, Bill and Fred were hired together.

Fred recalls:

It was when St. Paul's opened that Bill and I got to work

together and to get to know each other. He was the Social Worker and I was the Orientation and Mobility Teacher at this residential Rehabilitation Center. In fact, all of the staff were sort of specialists and we were pleased that Father Carroll had selected us to become a team of specialists.

Bill and I had to learn to Fence so that our clients could learn to use their other senses to live with Blindness. This brought the two of us together and we became a couple of specialists because we, in a sense, trained the Fencing Instructor. This also helped the two of us to have a good working relationship. I was amazed at his skill as a Counselor and I discovered from him, a lot of things that helped me to do a better job of teaching. For example, it was to our advantage if we could know the Trainee as well as possible. One technique that he used in his counseling that helped him to know that the person being counseled was uncomfortable was to have that person sit on a chair that would squeak if the person squirmed. That –put together with the subject being discussed, helped him help the client.

I think that his legacy to the blind community was to be a living example. He lived his life facing the same things that people in general faced in life. He got cold, he got wet, he had family troubles, he had to work full time, as did the rest of the staff. He got no special treatment because of his blindness. He had to keep his feelings out of the counseling sessions, and to conduct the session in a manner that made the client feel that he or she was the most important person in that room.

He also had to govern himself as just another staff person during our Group Therapy sessions. As a member of that staff, I can report that we reacted to him the same as we reacted to each other. We, including him, learned that we had to be free of any baggage that would interfere with helping our Trainees to be the person that they were, who just happened to be blind.

Bill was quite skillful in moving about as a blind person. In fact, two occasions come to mind about how at ease I felt about moving around with him. The first had to do with him and I going to work one morning on a crowded streetcar. Our stop was near the end of the line, so that we were able to get seats before we got to the stop. Bill got seated in a seat where the aisle of the car was at his right side. He must have felt comfortable enough or tired enough to go to sleep. About three or four blocks before our stop, the streetcar had to make a sharp turn to the left, which it did with some speed, and the torque of the car pulled Bill out of his seat onto the floor of the car. He was not hurt, but you can imagine the surprise this was for him and for me. I was not close enough to stop him from falling off the set. He and I thought the situation was funny. We had to convince the other passengers that he was Okay.

The other event where his skill got him into trouble was when I bought a house. I took some of my fellow workers and Bill to see the house. The house was built on a small hill. This was not bad because my garage was at the same level as the street. It took up part of the space in the basement of the house. This made it easy to enter the house through the garage, into the basement and when we were ready to see the rest of the house, we would go up the stairs from the basement to the kitchen. The house was a small ranch house so the living area was on a level above the garage. Well, I opened the garage and we went in and Bill had no trouble following us in. The problem occurred when Bill bumped his head on the stairway, which the rest of us had stooped to go under in order to see the rest of the basement. He called out to us and we told him that if he wasn't so skillful, we might have warned him about the stairs. Thank goodness he did not hurt himself. That tells how he functioned with us.

✳✳✳✳✳✳✳✳✳✳✳✳✳✳✳✳✳✳✳✳✳✳✳✳

One of the saddest chapters in Bill Gallagher's life was his first marriage, which took place in September 1950 at St. Mary's Catholic Church in Dedham, Massachusetts. The name of his first wife is not known, but friends remember that the couple had one son, William, whose nickname was Billy Mike. The marriage quickly went sour and ended in divorce. According to Richard

O'Keefe, Rocks told him that his wife had physically attacked him on more than one occasion. Because he was blind, he couldn't defend himself against her blows. He also suspected that she was unfaithful to him and that the child she bore was not his. After they separated, his wife and child moved away, perhaps to California, where she is thought to have remarried. Bill petitioned for an annulment, which was granted. Other friends report that Rocks met the child when the boy was a teenager and they spent a day together fishing in the Boston area.

A very happy chapter, however, was Bill's marriage to Catherine O'Brien, nicknamed Kay, whom he met when he was working in Boston in 1954 and living at the Buckminster Hotel in Kenmore Square in Boston. In those years, the Hotel Buckminster was a well known place, where all manner of famous and infamous people met and lived. Some of the famous personages who lived in or visited the Hotel regularly over the years included the great Bambino, Babe Ruth, who stayed in the Hotel when he was a member of the Boston Red Sox and later when he played for the New York Yankees. The great Red Sox hitter, Ted Williams was a regular visitor, as were members of all the visiting major league baseball teams when they were playing the Boston Red Sox in Fenway. During World War II, Italian prisoners of war were housed there.

One of the features of the hotel, aside from the cheap prices, was the Candlelight Room, a bar and lounge and gathering place for ballplayers, bookies, prostitutes, and all manner of people who attended local schools or worked in the area. Damon Runyan would have felt right at home at the Buckminster bar, where rare characters of all stripes gathered, laughed, drank and conspired to make all sorts of nefarious plans. One such plan hatched there was the historic 1919 Black Sox Baseball scandal. A decade later, the Buckminster was the site of the first radio network broadcast in 1929.

A lifelong friend, Bob Johnson, first met Bill at the Buckminster just after returning from the Korean War in 1954 and entering Boston University. Bob and five other veterans rented a suite of rooms at the Buckminster Hotel for a real bargain - $250.00 per month. The suite included three bedrooms, a kitchen, a bathroom and a living room. At this time, the Buckminster was renting rooms to all comers on a daily basis, for the week, month or even for four hours. Bob recalls those years as years of fun and frolic and parties every weekend.

A casual friend of Bill's from growing up in Maynard, Paul Batulin, became reacquainted with Bill through mutual friends at the hotel. Paul, too, has many fond memories of Bill and his days at the Buckminster. He recalls that Bill loved the atmosphere in the Hotel's bar with the smoke-filled chatter about sports, the ponies, odds on football games, long shots, the fights, and some clandestine deals, real or imagined.

One of the regular patrons of the bar was a well preserved middle aged woman, rumored to be Ted Williams' girlfriend. Paul happened to sit next to her at the bar one day, and engaged her in a conversation. At one point, he said: "I understand that you are a friend of Ted Williams." She responded, "Indeed, I am." Whereupon, she opened her purse and showed Paul a picture of Williams decked out in his Air Force uniform.

During his stay at the Buckminster, Bill invited his mother to come to the hotel for a visit. After several days, Mrs. Gallagher said to Rocks: "I notice in that apartment next to yours, a lot of men keep coming and going in and out of the apartment. What could they be up to?"

Rocks said to his mother with a big smile on his face: "There must be some kind of business going on there of a clandestine nature."

Catherine O'Brien, Bill's second wife, also lived at the Buckminster Hotel. Born in Marlboro, Massachusetts, Catherine was employed as the head nurse in charge of the recovery room at Boston City Hospital, and taught nursing on a college level. She moved into an apartment at the Buckminster with two other nurses, who like her had served in the Korean War on the front lines. Catherine returned as a second lieutenant and continued her service in the Army Reserve Corps until just before the Vietnam War, at which time she was honorably discharged with the rank of captain.

It was on a visit to Rocks at the Buckminster that Paul first met Catherine and her roommate, Peg. Thereafter, they often went out together on double dates. Eventually, Rocks married Catherine. Paul was his best man. Several years later, Paul married Peg and Bill was his best man. As Paul put it, after these two marriages, "the saga of the happy bachelors came to an end."

Paul had fond memories of Catherine: "She was a good girl – loved to kid around – if a risqué story was told, she might give a little hell to the story teller. She was not the glamorous type – did not spend much time in the beauty salons trying to make herself more beautiful – would not blow a lot of money on clothes or makeup, like some women do in these modern times."

Tom Sullivan recalls Catherine as trim and very pretty, with dark hair and a matter of fact manner. He says, "She always had an eye out for Billy's safety, but not to such an extent that she would take away any of his independence." Where Bill was concerned, Kay always remained in the background, letting Bill have the center of the stage. But she was always right there to support her Bill when and if he needed it.

****

After Bill had worked for about five years at St. Paul's, Father Carroll offered him a position as Chief of Professional Services at the headquarters of the Catholic Guild for All the Blind in Boston. He worked at this position for about three years. In 1961, Bill was invited to go to Pittsburgh by Gordon Connor, who had worked at St. Paul's and then moved on to direct the Greater Pittsburgh Guild for the Blind. Connor asked him to help set up a rehabilitation program in Pittsburgh similar to that at St. Paul's. Bill viewed it "as an exciting prospect – an opportunity to spread the Carroll philosophy about blindness."

Rocks: The Blind Guy at the Lake

When Bill Gallagher was leaving the Catholic Guild for the Blind in Newton, Massachusetts, to accept a position with the Greater Pittsburgh Guild for Blind in 1961, there was a testimonial dinner given for him. At that dinner, the Reverend Thomas J. Carroll, Rocks best friend and mentor, gave the following inspirational speech:

> *It's always nice to have a newspaper headline for a story. Some wag in the Guild office found one – and the headline is now on the office bulletin board: BIG DAY NEARS FOR PITTSBURGH.*

> *As all of you know by now, we're here because the Pirates got Bill Gallagher. There was no player exchange – no straight trade – just a straight cash deal. And we haven't seen the cash yet!*

> *The day of the last series game, I was flying from St. Louis to New York. The jet was about 20,000 feet up. It was a beautiful day up above the high overcast and as smooth as a jet can be. But the game was almost over and through the break in the clouds, you could almost feel the turbulence over the stadium.*

> *Pittsburgh may be looking forward to a great day. But so is Bill Gallagher. It's a good many years now since a younger Gallagher trekked off toward the West and pitched his wigwam on the West Bank of the meandering Blackstone. True Bostonian that he has become, he knows that other rivers lie somewhere beyond it – the Connecticut, which is a kind of outer barrier – and somewhere beyond the*

Rocks: The Blind Guy at the Lake

Connecticut, the Hudson, often confused by Bostonians with the Great Divide. Now, this Maynard-born and Worcester-bred Bostonian, who, until recently thought of Pittsburgh only in connection with boiler-makers, is on his way to far, far off Pennsylvania. Not to Philadelphia, that faint distant reflection of proper Boston. Not to Harrisburg, whose domed capital one thinks of as overlooking the Pacific, but over a longer trail to a town where three far-off rivers meet, where miners tunnel deep underground and golden buildings beckon. It's a long way from home, Bill, but you'll soon make yourself at home there. You'll own half the town. And if this were a night for predicting, I would say that the favorite beverage would be boiler-makers on the Rocks.

(I suppose after that one, somebody will suggest that this might be entitled 'Corn-on-the-Rocks.').

I would like to strike a little more serious note. I do see Bill Gallagher's trip to Pittsburgh as an important step. It is almost seven years since St. Paul's Rehabilitation Center for the Blind was founded in Newton. Seven years to the day on March 1, 1961, Pittsburgh will open another rehabilitation center founded on the plan of St. Paul's and destined to carry the philosophy of St. Paul's to new territory.

This may sound strange to you: But I see the founding of the Greater Pittsburgh Rehabilitation Center like a founding of the second chapter of a dream of N.A.A.B.P. – National Association for the Advancement of Blind Persons.

It is this concept that I would like to talk to you about tonight – the analogy of blindness in a sighted society to color in a white society – the comparison of prejudice against the blind with racial prejudice – the concept of the blind as a minority group.

Our statistics are not certain. There are 8,500, at most 12,000 blind persons in Massachusetts by any definition of blindness. In the United States, there are 350,000 – in the broadest definition 960,000. Compared with the total population of the State, or of the United States, these figures are small. Blind persons are a small minority group.

But small or large, it is a minority group. And it is subject to all the prejudice, the bias, the bigotry, that other minority groups are subject to. And segregation is as much a loaded word in our field as outside it – as much a thing to be opposed, contradicted, and fought against.

If there is one thing that St. Paul's Rehabilitation Center stands for, it is a fight against segregation, a fight for the integration of blind persons into a sighted society. It is this fight that has been a major part of Bill Gallagher's work since he came to the Guild for the Blind. And, it will be a major part of his work as he moves into new territory in Pittsburgh.

What is the comparison of blindness with color? The color of a man's skin in itself is no handicap. Whatever his race, it is something for him to glory in (except when he becomes ashamed of the fact that it is stooping to persecute others). Color in itself is not handicap – but a race-conscious white society can make it such.

Blindness, on the other hand, is a major and multiple handicap. Yet, a massive portion of the sighted world – a world which, too, often seeks to handle the problems of blindness by handouts and hand-me-downs for people who are blind – a world which excludes blind persons from its social life and from its economic life – which seeks to salve its conscience by establishing segregated recreation groups, segregated workshops, and segregated homes for those who are blind. It is a world afraid of blindness, as of all things unknown – afraid to come close to blindness, to touch it, to know it.

It's strange. You get the hopeful feeling that the world is growing up – and then you run again into a stupidity of prejudice. Last night, I was late getting to sleep. I had the radio on beside my bed, and I heard the Jerry Williams program. The topic was prejudice – I don't know if any of you heard it – but one particular stupid, ignorant, prejudiced woman was speaking of the shortcomings of the colored race. She was defending prejudice, and one particular quotation stays with me: 'You think it's only the uneducated, but I got a college education, and I have seen it myself – I have seen it with my own eyes.' Oh, the sickening ignorance. She was sure that Negroes wanted to live in poor quarters. That they could move elsewhere, but they'd rather spend their money on big cars. Another caller felt that colored people had their privileges and didn't live up to them. Down through the decades came the echoes of the same words that applied in Boston to the Irish, later to the Italians, and on to every minority group.

I am not here tonight to talk about the horror of race prejudice, either in the segregation of a Southern school, or the hidden Jim Crow in a suburban real estate office. But, I am here to remind you that in this and many areas where the "No Irish Need Apply" sign has been taken down, equivalent barriers still exist against other groups. There may be no sign that says, "No Blind People Need Apply" – but there is a wall of misunderstanding, which excludes them. There is a failure in all too many places to recognize that (it is so simple as almost to be meaningless) people are people. White people are people. Colored people are people. Sighted people are people. Blind people are people. Does it sound stupid? Perhaps it does, but it is basic! And until they are accepted, all of them as individual human beings, prejudice will continue to exist. The vicious circle of segregation and exclusion will continue to take its toll in the majority group and the minority group alike.

You are here tonight – we are here – to honor Bill Gallagher. If you know him well, then you know he does not meet the stereotype of the blind person, anyone of the stereotypes. He hasn't any sixth or seventh sense – has four senses and he has learned to use them well. If you thought of blind persons as musicians, he has certainly disabused you – he can't even carry a tune. And if you thought of blind persons as beggars, then I vouch for the fact that you got this one wrong. He is not "wonderful" or "amazing" in any magic sense. Instead, he is a person, a friend, who has done an outstanding job in overcoming the handicaps of blindness. And he is one who has helped others to do the same.

As an individual, and in his professional capacity, his job has been, and will be, to overcome prejudice, to replace ignorance with understanding, and unreasoning fear with intelligent insight.

Those of you who are truly his friends, will be fighting at his side, not in Pittsburgh, but wherever you meet prejudice. The help of everyone is needed because the job is vast. And neither the N.A.A.C.P., nor my mythical N.A.A.B.P., will ever meet their objective until the human race is associated for the advancement of all human beings.

Godspeed the day.

****

It was at this point in their lives that Bill and Kay decided to marry. They were married in Salem, New Hampshire in 1961 and then traveled to Pittsburgh as Mr. and Mrs. Gallagher.

****

WORKING IN PITTSBURGH

Bill's work at the Greater Pittsburgh Guild for the Blind included training the professional staff, hiring new staff, establishing new rehabilitation services, interviewing clients, administering a program serving five states, fund raising, public relations and public education activities. Eventually, Bill became director of the Guild. He recalled:

> *Throughout my tenure in Pittsburgh, I tested Carroll's book and philosophy. Doing so in a new territory proved exciting. The Carroll philosophy was expressed best in his book, Blindness: What It Is, What It Does, and How to Live with It. Carroll's thesis was that an adult who becomes blind loses not only sight but also loses 20 specific things related to it. The job of the rehabilitation center program, he believed, was to restore or find a substitution for each one of these losses. The identification of '20 losses,[1]' as Carroll's concept became popularly known, was the result of Carroll's comprehensive analysis of blindness derived from more than 20 years of study and experimentation.*

> *As Carroll saw it, a good rehabilitation program included two main components: instruction and counseling. The instruction was based on*

---

[1] See Addenda for listing and explanation of these twenty losses.

sensory training designed to ensure that a blind person gets full use of the other senses in order to make the best use of skills such as communication, orientation and mobility, and techniques of daily living. He believed strongly that the development of sensory training was even more important than learning the proper use of a cane. The second part of the Carroll rehabilitation program involved counseling on both the individual and the group level. In a nutshell, this is the program he put into practice at St. Paul's Rehabilitation Center, where it was highly effective.

Father Carroll came to Pittsburgh at various times to help with in-service training because we had a brand-new staff. Rather than lecture, Carroll preferred to be a group leader in a dynamic group setting. He worked hard on staff so that they would know not only their disciplines but also their true feelings about blindness and blind persons. He believed that group therapy was extremely important for the staff and, consequently, held a group meeting at St. Paul's once a week with an outside psychiatrist or psychologist leading the group. We did the same in Pittsburgh with good results.

In hiring new employees, Carroll wanted first to know how sincere the applicant was in his or her commitment. He probed the individual in order to discover his or her attitude toward blindness and to see how comfortable he or she was in talking about blindness. The individual's response weighed more heavily with Carroll than his or her educational background or prior work experience. Having seen how well this approach worked for Father Carroll, I adopted it myself in Pittsburgh and still consider it the best way to assemble a staff of top-notch people.

****

During his tenure at the Rehabilitation Center, Greater Pittsburgh Guild for the Blind, there was an article in "This Week in Pittsburgh," a weekly magazine on what was going on in Pittsburgh, entitled "This Week's Personality," dated September 25, 1964:

> *William F. Gallagher, director of The Rehabilitation Center, Greater Pittsburgh Guild for the Blind, lost his sight at age 15.*

> *'It is a terrible loss,' he readily admits, 'but it is certainly not the worst tragedy that can strike a human being.'*

> *Mr. Gallagher's belief that normal life and activity can be resumed after blindness led him to complete his high school work at Perkins School for the Blind and to go on to take degrees at Holy Cross College and Boston College.*

> *A member of the Academy of Certified Social Workers, this native of Maynard, Massachusetts, served as a social worker for the Boston Child Welfare Department and as a supervisor of social services at St. Paul Rehabilitation Center, Newton, Massachusetts, before coming to The Rehabilitation Center in Shadyside three years ago. Mr. Gallagher also teaches in the Graduate School Department of Special Education and Rehabilitation at the University of Pittsburgh.*

> *He has published articles in 'The New*

Rocks: The Blind Guy at the Lake

Outlook for the Blind' and 'The Home Teacher,' a Brailled magazine. A nationally known figure in the field of blindness and rehabilitation, Mr. Gallagher annually addresses numerous conventions and conferences.

Another article in the magazine entitled, 'Mobility for the Blind' which covered one of the aspects of Bill's work while he served as Director of The Rehabilitation Center Greater Pittsburgh Guild for the Blind is as follows:

Seeing a blind person travel independently still causes people to gasp and gape a little. Some even suspect a magical sixth sense is at work when a blind person successfully crosses a street, avoiding running into a utility pole or doesn't trip off a curb.

Any blind person who takes the 15 week course at the Rehabilitation Center Greater Pittsburgh Guild for the Blind will tell a different story, though so will the many blind men and women who have learned mobility in their homes and communities throughout the Guild's Community Network Program.

Mobility, the prized possession of the toddler who finally learns to take two steps without a tumble, is one of the most serious losses a newly blinded person suffers. It is not easily restored. And the blind person cannot count on any automatic sensory compensation or sixth sense. It simply is not there.

There is more to mobility than handing a blind person a cane, patting him on the back and telling him to take off. This method is more dangerous than helpful. Trainees at the Shadyside Center learn to travel safely and independently in residential and even heavily commercial areas using the long cane and their trained remaining senses.

In teaching use of the cane with the proper technique, the Guild's mobility specialists also train the remaining senses of the blind person. These senses must become information collectors for the blinded person – telling him things he once could find out using his sight.

Mobility is one of the 24 courses the Rehabilitation Center offers. Some others, deal with visualization (a great aid to orientation for blinded adults), techniques of daily living – eating, shaving, applying make-up, pouring coffee, communications – handwriting, typing, Braille and such unspoken aids to communication as teaching the blind person to look at a sighted person when talking and react with various expressions.

Courses and counseling also investigate the blind person's attitude about being blind, and aid the individual toward recovering from the tragedy of blindness by learning to live successfully with his handicap.

Five years old this month, The Greater Pittsburgh Guild works in all its services toward an integrated life for blind men and women – working – working and socializing with sighted friends and associates.

****

While Bill Gallagher was at the Greater Pittsburgh Guild for the Blind, he was interviewed by Frank Berkopec of the United Press International in Pittsburgh, Pennsylvania on the importance of fencing as an aid to a blind person. Frank wrote:

> *Two fencers. . . masks and body protectors in place. . . . assume the classic stance. At a command they begin. Their foils ring on contact and it is the only sound except for an occasional stamp of a foot on the tile floor.*

> *After a short time the fencing master, standing off to one side, shouts a command: 'Raise the arm higher.' As the fencers maneuver, other commands are shouted. . . keep your head up.'*

> *The fencers respond. . . but occasionally the head of one tends to drop a bit. Again the shouted command.*

> *'That's the way it is with a newly-blinded adult' explains 38-year old Bill Gallagher. They become shy and withdrawn and the first place it tells is in the position of the head, regardless of what they are doing.*

> *Gallagher, who is blind himself, is assistant director of rehabilitation at the Greater Pittsburgh Guild for the Blind. It's one of two places in the United States where the blind learn fencing. The other is at Newton, Massachusetts.*

> *Gallagher tells his story this way: 'I went to bed one night with 20-20 vision and when I got up the next morning, I was blind. I was 15 years old. Something happened to the optic nerve. . . something mysterious and rare.'*

As part of his rehabilitation, Bill learned fencing. He says it taught him balance, coordination and proper body position, which is what others learn at the Pittsburgh Center.

He explains: 'We use the classical method of fencing to teach the adult blind. It is based on touch which is very important to a blind person. Fencing teaches a certain amount of aggressiveness and quick reactions.'

He explains further: 'The newly blinded persons tend to slouch. Fencing teaches him to stand erect and keep his head up. It teaches him awareness . . . like the closeness of the opposition. And above all it teaches him the proper position of the head.'

Bill says from the contact of the foils, the blind person can transfer this sense of touch to the cane. Through fencing he also learns to adjust to sound. A cane tapping on a sidewalk naturally makes a different sound than one tapping on a boardwalk.

Bill says blind persons usually are nervous about learning fencing 'but they soon get over that,' he says. 'You see, we don't think that blindness is darkness.'

****

John and Anne Kelly were two of the closest friends that Bill Gallagher ever had. Their friendship began in 1962 in Pittsburgh.

John and Anne were living in a very poor section of Pittsburgh. They were barely eking out a living. John had graduated from the University of Scranton in 1955, spent two years in the United States Army and worked as a pharmaceutical salesman until 1962, when he decided to go to Pharmacy School at the University of Pittsburgh. Anne worked as a full-time nurse.

It was customary for John, on Saturdays, to go to the Laundromat in Shadyside, a more affluent part of Pittsburgh, where he felt more comfortable. At this time, while he attended Pharmacy School, he worked on the side in a drug store.

One Saturday in 1962, John went to his favorite Laundromat – put his laundry in the washing machine, followed by the necessary number of nickels, dimes and quarters.

As was his wont, he then went to a bar and restaurant next door for a few beers, while the washing machine worked away. The name of the place was Mitchell's Steak House.

The television set was on showing a football game – Army v. Holy Cross. John was rooting for Holy Cross, since it was a Jesuit institution, like his own University of Scranton.

There was a stranger sitting at the bar next to John, who was also rooting for Holy Cross. Sooner than later, they were engaged in a friendly conversation. The stranger's name was Bill Gallagher.

At first, John had no idea that Bill was blind. At one point, the bartender placed two glasses of beer in front of the men. John noticed that Bill was feeling for his glass, which he thought strange. A little while later, Bill had to go to the men's room. He had left his jacket hanging on the back of the bar stool. It was then that John noticed a blind man's cane, neatly folded up in the inside pocket of Bill's jacket.

By and by, Bill's wife, Kay, entered the bar with a grocery bag on wheels. The three of them engaged in a friendly spirited conversation. John learned, at this time, that Bill was the head man at The Greater Pittsburgh Build for the Blind.

At that meeting, the seeds of a wonderful friendship were

planted, a friendship that was to last unbroken for 38 years.

Thereafter, a pattern was established. John met Kay and Bill, same time, same day, same place. It was not too long after that Anne Kelly joined the threesome.

These Saturday meetings evolved into meeting the Gallaghers at their home once a week. The Gallaghers invited many of their friends over to join the festivities, which included eating and drinking and, most of all, singing. There was not a popular old song or a popular new song that John did not know by heart. He had a melodious and willing voice that filled the night with song and everyone joined in. You might be sure that one of the songs that John would sing during the evening would be Mamie Reilly, one of Rock's favorites. (Yale undergraduates have the Whiffenpoof song. Holy Cross has Mamie Reilly.) These parties went on for about three years until Bill received an offer to join the New York Association For the Blind, a/k/a The Lighthouse in New York, New York. This was an offer that Bill could not refuse. The year was 1965.

John remembers, "The Gallaghers came to the Christening of our first child at our home. It was not much of a place. In fact, it was a dump. Bill must have had that in his mind when he was moving to New York City. He was an extraordinarily kind person. He gave us some beautiful furniture and wonderful rugs for our bare floors."

There was a time during the Pittsburgh years, when Bill and John Kelly were at the Moose Club, a private club for men, during a social night out. John recalls, "Who walked over to greet Bill but Bill Mazeroski, one of the all time baseball heroes in the history of the Pittsburgh Pirates. It was Mazeroski who hit the winning home run that defeated the New York Yankees in the World Series final game. Frankly, not being a baseball fan at that time, I did not know Mazeroski from a hole in the ground, but in my conversation with him, I pretended to know who he was and what he had done. Gallagher got the drift of this and after Mazeroski left, he laid into me: "You did not know that man from Adam. You just pretended you knew him, you old joker." He often joked about this incident down through the years."

On a more serious note, John states, "Bill loved to go to Forbes Field in Pittsburgh to see the Pirates play baseball. I often accompanied him and was able to describe to him what was going on in the game.

When we went to the game, before we entered Forbes Field, Bill would ask me, "Are there any blind beggars with tin cups in the area?" There always were a few. He would then ask me to lead him to such a person or persons. Bill would then speak to each one of these blind men individually. In essence, he would speak to them in a kind, but firm voice as follows: "My name is Bill. I am a blind man just like yourself. I can help you to give up this begging with your tin cup and make you a self-reliant person, if you will, but give me a chance."

More often than not, the blind person would accept Bill's offer. Bill explained to me that the program at the Guild would help the blind man to do ordinary chores on his own. He would be taught to get around by using a cane. As time went on, the blind person would be able to walk around a building with a sighted person in tow. Later on, they would walk from place to place, crossing at intersections. The purpose was to give the blind person confidence in his ability to walk from place to place.

When the teacher felt that the blind person was able to go it on his own, he would be so advised and told that he was sufficiently advanced to go on his own. Off went the blind man on his great adventure. Little did he know or suspect that his teacher was never far away from him, in case some emergency developed.

As time went on, the blind person, having learned his lessons well, was able to complete his journey all by himself, full of confidence that he had built up in himself.

A small miracle had taken place.

The tin cup was put in storage forever."

John continued his account of what Bill told him: "There are, of course many other facets to the training regimen, which includes teaching the blind person how to dress and undress, personal hygiene, how to cook and eat, keep this room neat and clean, how to use Braille, how to type,, et al.

One of the immediate goals of the program was to get jobs for the blind person, e.g., dry cleaning. The idea was to make the blind person independent – to give him self-esteem, to be self-sufficient enough so that he would not be dependent on others."

When Bill was departing Pittsburgh for New York, he was given a big testimonial dinner. Present at the affair was Bishop Wright, the Mayor of the City of Pittsburgh, all the leading legislators from the region, professional people and just average "Joes," who had come under Bill's spell in his Pittsburgh years.

When Bill rose to speak, he admonished those in attendance–

> *There are too many blind beggars in Pittsburgh.
> These and people like them, we can help at the
> Greater Pittsburgh Guild for the Blind. We can
> build their self-esteem and help to integrate them
> into society. All we need is a chance to do the job.
> With your help, it will be done.*

The headlines in the Pittsburgh newspapers the next day stated:

Too many Blind Beggars in Pittsburgh.
We Can Help.
Give Us A Chance.

Throughout his life, certain stereotypes of blind people bothered Bill. One such stereotype of a blind person that upset him was the blind beggar with the tin cup because he knew that the blind person was far more capable of doing greater things with his life.

THE LIGHTHOUSE

After five years in Pittsburgh, Bill Gallagher moved on to the New York Association for the Blind, the Lighthouse, becoming the Director of a newly named Department of Rehabilitation Services in May 1965. The Lighthouse, founded in 1905, had a long history of services for blind people that had evolved with the increasing recognition of the need to provide work opportunities for blind people, education for blind children, and with new advances in technology, increased recognition of the importance of maximizing partial sight. The Lighthouse had gone through many organizational changes, and in 1965, after a major management study that put the focus of Lighthouse programs on rehabilitation, Bill Gallagher arrived to develop rehabilitation based on the philosophy of Father Thomas Carroll.

Bill made many progressive changes. There was an old division known as "Vocational Rehab Services." Bill changed the name to this division to "Rehab Services," which then included new programs and new approaches. These changes included a diagnostic program which took four weeks, rehabilitation training which lasted from eight to sixteen weeks depending on the ability of each individual, and vocational training which included classes in communication skills, Braille, typing, eye contact and how to comport oneself. A psychologist was on the staff and counseling was available.

Arlene Gordon, who had preceded Bill at The Lighthouse by a few months as head of the Children and Adolescent Services, recalls that Bill brought in a highly skilled staff of psychologists, orientation and mobility instructors, and other rehabilitation specialists.

During the time Arlene worked at The Lighthouse, she lost her own vision. Reflecting on her own blindness, and how she handled it, she said, "Knowing Bill Gallagher was probably what helped me the most to get through losing my sight when it happened so precipitously. I knew that life goes on; that independent living is possible. Bill was a wonderful role model."

In a poignant moment of recollection, the last time that Arlene saw Bill was very shortly before she became totally blind. Her vision was blurry. Bill was standing under a ceiling spotlight in the Executive Suite at The Lighthouse. Arlene said to him, "I can just about see your face." She then added, "I never saw a human face again."

After Bill left The Lighthouse in 1972 to go to The American Foundation for the Blind, he and Arlene maintained their friendship over the ensuing years. Arlene retired from The Lighthouse in 1990 but remains associated with it and active as a member of the Board of Directors – a woman who, in her retirement, is still hale and hearty and full of boundless energy.

Arlene recalled one incident of Bill's wit: Bill attended a seminar in Dallas, Texas, with another member of The Lighthouse. After the seminar, they boarded a plane in Dallas to return to New York. There were three seats, side-by-side. A woman sat in the window seat. Bill had his cane with him, so the woman undoubtedly knew he was blind.

The plane took off and was flying for about five minutes, when the woman said to Bill, "I wonder how high up we are." Bill answered, "We are now flying at 25,000 feet."

The woman was completely astounded. She said, "Oh, that's marvelous. You are able to sense that."

In telling Arlene about this incident, he ended the story by saying, "I did not bother to tell her that the captain, just a few seconds before the woman had spoken to him had announced: "Ladies and gentlemen, we are traveling at a height of 25,000 feet."

Rocks: The Blind Guy at the Lake

****
THE ELBOW HAS AN INTELLIGENCE QUOTIENT
BY: WILLIAM F. GALLAGHER
OCTOBER 1969

"Would you like to take my elbow?" is the question a sighted person should ask when offering assistance to a blind person at a street crossing, or when he intends to guide a blind person in the direction he wishes to walk. The blind person should be advised to take the sighted person's elbow and walk about half a step behind his guide, whether crossing the street, traveling along the sidewalk, or going up or down stairs. The blind person should have a gentle, but firm grip, just above the elbow of the sighted person. When this procedure is followed, the two persons may travel comfortably with assuredness and safety, and carry on a conversation at the same time.

If the sighted person offers assistance in a manner which is not what the blind person wants, he should inform the sighted person concerning the proper technique, quietly and quickly. Sighted persons, who are not familiar with blindness, naturally do not know correct techniques, and, it is therefore, the full responsibility of the blind person to educate the person who has offered to help him.

A competent blind person finds elbows fascinating, revealing, and almost talkative. The first touch of the elbow, tells the blind person whether the sighted person is nervous, frightened, or at ease. Some sighted persons are very uncomfortable when they meet a blind person for the first time, and this information is communicated through an unbending, rigid elbow. A relaxed, non-trembling elbow, indicates that the sighted person is comfortable with the blind person.

The elbow gives away the height, weight, and shape. This last statistic is gauged through the relationship of the elbow to the hip. A blind person can gauge height from soundings of the voice and by using his own height as a measuring stick. As one clasps a generously rounded elbow that fills the grip, if the sound of the voice comes from below, the blind person knows that the one offering assistance is short, and could be quite stocky. If the elbow is sharp and bony, and the voice comes from above, one visualizes a tall, thin person.

The elbow of a woman, can tell the blind person whether she is completely feminine or leans towards some masculine traits – just through the softness, smoothness, or roughness and hardness of the skin. Dainty movements and gait may serve to indicate femininity, but jerky movements and a long, bold stride, may suggest masculine traits. If the blind person is a woman, she can visualize through her touch at the elbow of the man assisting her, whether he is strong, athletic, robust, or of delicate physique. Be mindful here, that his tailor may mislead her through false elbow pads! The texture of the garment can help fill in the picture.

Age can be perceived at the elbow through its dominant characteristics of wrinkles, flabby folds, uneven surfaces, and a touch of trembling. The elbow of youth, has a jaunty spring with its step and wears a soft, tight, smooth skin.

The elbow is a sophisticated communicative device regarding the personality of the individual. A lazy, limp dropped elbow may reveal that the person is one who seldom smiles and shows little facial expression, whereas a lively, moving elbow may indicate an animated personality and expressive face. The elbow can manifest warmth and a genuine sincerity or a cool aloofness.

An elbow with a high I.Q. can be extremely helpful to the blind person. It gives good clues as to when to slow down, or walk faster. When to turn left or right, when to weave in and out of crowds, when to step behind the guide in order to follow through a narrow pathway, when to step up and step down, when a landing is reached, and it can make the blind person aware that people are approaching. The blind person can easily get the message from a well-trained elbow that it has already been thoroughly educated in the manner of assisting blind persons.

Rocks: The Blind Guy at the Lake

The elbow, in and by itself, is stripped of prejudice and accepts the person as he is. It raises itself to guide, unencumbered by curiosity to identify the religion, race, or background of the blind person. And, finally, it can be helpful in breaking down some of the emotional barriers that oft times stand between blind persons and sighted persons.

If, heretofore, you thought that an elbow is a nondescript part of one's anatomy, it is hoped that you now know better. The elbow can be a fascinating, sometimes beautiful and always, an informational piece of the human structure.

THE CARROLL CENTER

In 1961, Father Carroll published a book on the rehabilitation of the blind that won international recognition: Blindness: What it is, What it Does, and How to Live with it (Little, Brown & Co.), hereinafter referred to as "Blindness". Translated into many languages, it has served to provide a model for many centers throughout the world. Bill Gallagher himself was the source of much of the information contained in Carroll's work.

Carroll's book provides a window to the heart and soul of the blind man and the awesome challenges that face the newly blinded person faces. He discusses the difference between congenital and adventitious blindness. A congenitally blind person is one who is blind from birth. An adventitiously blind person is one who becomes blind at some later stage in his life. From Father Carroll's perspective, this book deals not so much "with poignancy of 'lack,' but rather with the pain of loss."

He wrote: It is the whole and unique person who receives the multiple blows and he receives it according to his own personality structure, his own way of life, his own interests and circumstances. Any analysis of the losses of blindness must be applied to each blinded person as an individual – as must the resulting program of rehabilitation.

"The Sighted Man Dies" is the heading in Chapter One. He explains:

When in the full current of his sighted life, blindness comes on a man, it is the end, the death of that sighted life. However it comes, it is death to a way of life that has become part of the man. It is the end of acquired methods of doing things, the loss of built up relationships with people, of ingrained relationships with an environment. It is a destructive blow to the self image, which a man has carefully, though unconsciously constructed throughout his lifetime, a blow almost to his being itself.

Father Carroll points out that there are "worse tragedies than this." Despair is not the answer to this tragedy, far from it. As Carroll phrases it:

> "For there is a new life ahead. But this is the paradox: the sighted person is 'dead,' the blind person who is born can, once more, become the same person, but only if he is willing to go through the pain of death to sight."

In Blindness, Carroll theorized that a person who becomes blind not only loses sight, but experiences 20 other physical, emotional and psychological 'losses.'[2] Those losses range from loss of confidence in the remaining senses and loss of ease in written communication to loss of self-esteem. The role of rehabilitation, according to Carroll, is to restore or provide a reasonable substitute for those losses.

Moreover, since the various losses affect different people in different ways, Carroll felt that rehabilitation programs should be tailored to meet individual needs. His ideas were based on information gathered during hundreds of informal conversations with blind people of all ages.

****

Always seeking to apply the latest in research to the needs of the blind, Father Carroll had founded the American Center for Research in Blindness and Rehabilitation in 1963. In 1965, underscoring his pioneer spirit and dedication to the problems of research and blindness, he convinced the archdiocese of Boston to close a home for Aged Blind Women and transformed it into a geriatric rehabilitation center which merged with the St. Paul's Center.

Father Carroll served on many national and international committees, including the President's Committee on Employment

---

[2] See Addenda for listing and explanation of the 20 losses.

of the Handicapped, and the Special Legislative Commission, which studied problems of blind children and their families in Massachusetts. He was the recipient of nearly 100 national and international honors in work for the blind, including an honorary L.L.D. degree from Holy Cross in 1966, the Bell Greve Memorial Award of the National Rehabilitation Association in 1960, and the Miguel Medal of AFB. He was the National Chaplain of the Blinded Veterans Association for twenty-five years, a member of the Presidents' Committee on Employment of the Physically Handicapped, the National Advisory Neurological Disease and Blindness Council, and the World Commission of Research in Rehabilitation.

Over many years, the lives of Bill Gallagher and Father Carroll became intertwined. In life, Father Carroll was Bill's mentor, but in truth, he was more than that. Bill and Father Carroll became great personal friends working side by side to advance the cause of the blind community. In effect, they showed the way how blind people could become fully integrated in a not always receptive world. They opened the doors of opportunity to the blind in a way that was never achieved or even imagined before in the history of mankind. Father Carroll and Bill Gallagher were two giants in the cause of the blind community in the Twentieth Century. Their great contributions in that noble cause have had and will have an everlasting effect on the opening of a new and productive world for the blind in this nation, and in the world at large.

Jacob Levine, Ph.D. said of Father Thomas Carroll:

> *"The many blind and sighted who know and love Father Carroll are aware of the psychological profundity of his work, of his dedication to his faith, and to the blind, and of his inspired influence upon so many individuals. But many of us, perhaps, do not fully appreciate the extent to which his creative ideas will influence work with the blind for years hence, because they are so fundamental, and at*

times, so revolutionary."

****

Father Carroll's untimely death occurred in 1971.

****

In the <u>AFB News</u>, Volume 25, Number 1, Joanne LaFrancois wrote an excellent article entitled "Remembering the Work of Father Thomas J. Carroll":

> *NEW YORK – "If I had to name those individuals who have profoundly shaped our system of helping people cope with vision loss, one person would top the list, Father Thomas J. Carroll. Indeed, Father Carroll was to blindness rehabilitation what Dr. Howard Rusk, of the renowned Rusk Institute, was to the field of medical rehabilitation."*

> *So says John F. Muldoon, Ph.D., executive director of Ravenswood Hospital Community Mental Health Center in Chicago, and a longtime admirer of the man who pioneered the notion that rehabilitation services for blind people should address psychological as well as physical needs.*

> *Dr. Muldoon has recently finished editing a series of papers by leaders in the blindness field entitled Essays on Blindness Rehabilitation in Honor of Thomas J. Carroll: A Festschrift.[3] Citing their*

---

[3] Much of what Bill Gallagher had to say about his friendship with Father Carroll in this book was taken from his essay 'Father Thomas J. Carroll: Mentor and Friend' from "<u>Blindness Rehabilitation in Honor of Thomas J. Carroll: A Festschrift</u>" (a volume of writings by different authors presented as a tribute or memorial, especially to a scholar).

impressions of Carroll and his work in the context of current issues impacting services for blind people, Dr. Muldoon notes that Carroll's ideals and aspirations are as relevant today as they were 30 years ago.

The Festschrift grew out of the T. J. Carroll Lecture Series, which was sponsored by AFB, the Blinded Veterans Association (BVA) and the Carroll Center for the Blind in Newton, MA, to mark several key anniversaries. Among them, the 40th anniversary of the founding of BVA, the 35th anniversary of the founding of the Carroll Center, the 25th anniversary of the publication of Carroll's landmark book, Blindness: What It Is, What It Does and How To Live With It, and the 15th anniversary of Carroll's death. 'It seemed a fitting way to pay tribute to a man who greatly influenced the philosophy and direction of services for blind people in the United States,' said Dr. Muldoon.

The article continued:

The Festschrift is divided into two parts. Part One focuses on personal reflections of Carroll and his theories. Part Two features professional commentaries on rehabilitation services. Among topics discussed by the authors are aging and blindness; losses and restorations in recreation, careers, vocational goals and financial security; use and misuse of technology; and advocacy as well as an overview of Carroll's contributions to the blindness system and to blind persons themselves.

Contributing authors include Dr. Muldoon; Robert Amendola, a sculptor who has been an instructor in videation and spatial orientation at the Carroll Center since 1954; Glenn Plunkett, AFB's governmental relations specialist; Priscilla Rogers, program administrator, Division of Blind Services, Florida Department of Education, Tallahassee; Lawrence Scadden, Ph.D., Director, Electronic Industries Foundation Rehabilitation Engineering Center, Washington, D.C., Susan J. Spungin, Ed.D., AFB's associate executive director for program services; and William Thompson, who served as BVA's executive director, national president, treasurer and in various other capacities until his death in 1988.

The Festschrift also features comments by Ronald L. Miller, Ph.D., executive director of the BVA, and Rachel Ethier Rosenbaum, executive director of the Carroll Center. In the foreword, Miller points out that Carroll 'was a champion not only for blind people, but also for all disabled people, for downtrodden and poverty-stricken people, and for people who are victims of racial discrimination.'

Dr. Muldoon wrote, "Carroll was a complex man whose work in the areas of social equity, rehabilitation and religious service was energized by his intense sense of justice and charity. Each of these essays examines one of Carroll's many facets and the end result is a composite portrait of a man who remains an example of commitment and public service."

****

Rocks: The Blind Guy at the Lake

In 1972, the Guild was renamed The Carroll Rehabilitation Center for the Visually Impaired to honor Father Carroll. The recovery by the Carroll Center after Carroll's death was due, in no small part, to Rachel Ethier Rosenbaum, who was called upon by the Board to take on the position of Executive Director. The challenge was great. However, Rosenbaum rose to it and today the Carroll Center is flourishing. In *The Festschrift,* she notes, "When I was named director of the Carroll Center I took on the task of sorting through Carroll's correspondence. It was then that I realized how broad and far-reaching his humanitarian activities were.' Carroll's noteworthy accomplishments included participating in Dr. Martin Luther King, Jr.'s civil rights march in Selma, AL, advocating liturgical reform in the Catholic Church in the 1960's, and helping to establish specialized services for multiply disabled blind people in Massachusetts."

Rosenbaum recalls:

When I was appointed Executive Director of the Carroll Center in 1976, I didn't know Bill Gallagher but was quite familiar with his name and his reputation as a very successful blind person. As Father Carroll's successor, I was also familiar with the strong relationship formed between Bill and Father Carroll.

When I became Executive Director, Bill was a VP, and the Director of Rehabilitation at the New York Lighthouse. Understanding that the Carroll Center's future was uncertain and knowing what Father Carroll had intended for his agency – he volunteered to come up with a colleague during Christmas week to give the staff a seminar on the Carroll Philosophy. I knew from that moment on that I could count on Bill whenever I needed help. And I did call on him many times since then both as a trusted friend and a colleague.

Bill and I shared many funny moments – once leaving a meeting in Mississippi, Bill suggested that we travel together to Boston – as we were on the same airline – by this time, I was so used to being around blind persons that I did not hover over them – and Bill's incredible mobility skills made me forget he was blind – so when we transferred in the Atlanta airport – I noted we had to leave a section of the airport to find the train transport to the next terminal – it was only as I entered the train that I noticed Bill was not at my side – so I retraced my steps and found Bill standing exactly where I left him – he said he figured sooner or later I would notice my lost "luggage."

On another occasion, after a session at the agency during which time Bill had come up again to assist us, we all went out to eat dinner at the nearby hotel restaurant. The waitress – not recognizing that Bill was blind said she could not stretch her arm out to hand the plate to the person sitting the farthest in the booth because some stupid blind man had left his cane sticking out from under his seat, tripped her, and caused her to dislocate her shoulder. The four of us had all we could do not to burst into laughter as we hurriedly looked down to assure ourselves that Bill did not have his cane sticking out from under the table.

One of my favorite stories is the one Bill told me about the day Father decided that there was no reason blind people could not roller skate, so he put skates on Bill – at 225 Franklin Street in downtown Boston near the offices of Catholic Charities and sent Bill off on the sidewalk, on his adventure. Soon Bill lost control and was out on the street screaming with Carroll running ahead; a tall (6'4") thin man in cassock trying to stop the traffic as Bill came barreling down the street on his skates. (Of course, traffic was considerably less in the early 1940's but still dangerous).

THE AMERICAN FOUNDATION FOR THE BLIND

Bill Gallagher first joined the American Foundation for the Blind ("AFB") in 1972, when he assumed responsibility for the AFB's programs. He became the fourth CEO of the AFB in 1980 and he served in that capacity until 1991. He remembered, "In 1972, the year after Father Carroll's death, I was invited to join the staff of AFB. I had been at the Lighthouse as director of rehabilitation for about seven and a half years, and although the opportunity to join AFB was exciting and challenging, I wished that Father Carroll was around. A couple of long drives in his car would have helped with my decision. To this day, as I plan and administer the large program at AFB, I miss those rides as I make decisions."

The AFB, the organization to which Helen Keller devoted her life, is a national nonprofit whose mission is to ensure that the ten million Americans who are blind or visually impaired enjoy the same rights and opportunities as other citizens. It promotes wide-ranging, systemic change by addressing the most critical issues facing the growing blind and visually impaired population – employment, independent living, literacy, and technology. In addition to its New York City headquarters, the AFB maintains four National Centers in cities across the United States, and a Governmental Relation office in Washington, D.C.

During her life, Helen Keller was one of the world's great heroes. Her remarkable story was well known throughout the world. Born in 1880, she contracted an illness when she was less than two years old that left her unable to hear or see. A passionate and determined advocate for other people with disabilities, Helen Keller began to work with the AFB in 1924. She served as a spokesperson and ambassador for the Foundation until her death in 1968.

A member of AFB's Board of Trustees from 1987 to 1991, Carl R. Augusto succeeded Bill when he retired, becoming President and Chief Executive Officer of the AFB in May of 1991. During his tenure, Augusto has guided AFB toward improved fiscal stability and greater focus in addressing critical issues facing the field of blindness. He has expanded AFB'S scope to influence corporate America to make products and services accessible to blind and visually impaired people and has brought organizations, of and for the blind, together toward common objectives and greater collaboration. He has published several articles within and outside of the blindness field and has received numerous honors and awards, including the Robert B. Irwin Award presented by National industries for the Blind for outstanding contributions to the employment of people who are blind.

Augusto remembers that Bill made many contributions to AFB and the blindness field during his forty year career. He lists three major initiatives that Bill launched that have had a lasting impact at AFB:

- *Until the late 70's, AFB had two offices, the headquarters in New York and a Governmental Relations office in Washington, D.C. Bill saw the need to establish offices throughout the country to help agencies and schools improve their services. So, regional offices were established in Atlanta, Chicago, Denver, and San Francisco. In 1981, the Denver office was relocated to Dallas. The staff in these offices focused on identifying agencies and schools in their region that needed management or programmatic assistance or consultation. They either provided the consultation or asked others within AFB to do so. Many agencies have attributed to AFB the impetus to make major changes to improve services. Statewide needs assessments were conducted and in several instances, organizations were merged to eliminate redundancies. One example was in Atlanta when an agency for African American and whites were merged into one.*

- *Bill recognized the promise that technology held for blind and visually impaired people. The technological revolution for the blind population started in the early 70's with the development of the Kurzwell reading machine which converted print into synthetic speech. Bill established a technology center at AFB which has grown and flourished since then. He wanted to develop technologically advanced products to sell to blind people, which AFB did for many years. He also wanted to test products designed for blind people and to establish a data base for blind people in North America that were working and using technology on the job. He saw this group of blind people as potentially serving as mentors or information sources to young blind people, parents, counselors, and teachers.*

- *There has been so much fractionalization within the blindness field. Organizations of and for the blind were fighting each other, diverting resources from assisting blind people, to the battleground. Bill felt this should stop. Very few of us in the blindness field at the time thought that there could be a rapprochement with one organization, the National Federation of the Blind, who seemed to oppose so many of the things that the rest of us in the blindness field believed in. Bill disagreed and started a long term effort to build trust between AFB and the National Federation of the Blind. Many positive initiatives were begun as a result. If it wasn't for Bill Gallagher, none of that would have happened. Bill was truly an optimist but proved on so many occasions that his optimism was really realism.*

Augusto remembers that Bill had three entities he loved: AFB, the Carroll Center for the Blind, and perhaps more than both of these, Holy Cross College. He states, "When Bill loved something, he put a great deal of energy into it. AFB is so very fortunate to have benefited from his leadership and contributions over the years. I know that the Carroll Center and Holy Cross feel the same way.

Bill Gallagher was a true humanitarian who was blessed

with an enormous appetite to give to others and contributed to the betterment of society. We miss his laughter, his enthusiasm, his optimism and his spirit."

****

In his position as AFB's Executive Director, Bill was called upon to do extensive public relations work. He appeared before Congress and other government bodies and agencies to speak on issues and legislation that had a direct influence on the blind community. Bill and Kay also traveled together all over the United States and the world, always on the business of the blind community. Their travels took them to Russia, Australia, England, and Ireland. John Kelly recalls that Bill revealed a little trick he had when he checked into a hotel room. On leaving his room, he would wrap a rubber band tightly around the door knob in such a way that the average person would not know that it was there. When he returned to his room, he felt for the rubber band to make sure that he had the proper room.

AFB Goes to Russia

By Fay Hava Jarosh

NEW YORK – A team of five professionals from the American Foundation for the Blind (AFB) returned recently from a whirlwind tour of the Soviet Union with a commitment to exchange information about low- and high-tech adapted devices for blind people and other education, rehabilitation and employment programs.

The group toured facilities for blind Soviets – in Moscow, Leningrad, Minsk, and Grodno – as guests of the All Russia Association for the Blind. The ten-day itinerary included visits to rehabilitation centers, schools for blind children and blindness professionals, factories for blind workers, talking book studios as well as cultural and social centers.

"We were overwhelmed by the warmth and hospitality of our Soviet hosts," said AFB Executive Director William F. Gallagher, who spearheaded the group. "Indeed, we hope to reciprocate, in turn, when professionals from the All Russia Association tour AFB and other U.S. blindness organizations in 1990."

Gallagher had received an invitation from the president of the All Russia Association, Alexandre Neumyvakin, in July 1988 during a meeting of the World Blind Union in Madrid.

Other members of the AFB delegation included Susan J. Spungin, Ed.D., associate executive director for program services; Saul Freedman, Ph.D., director of national services in aging and blindness; Gerald Miller, director of national services in employment and rehabilitation training, and Elliot Schreier, director of the National Technology Center.

In separate interviews, AFB participants shared their observations about the Soviet blindness system. Gallagher was impressed by the professional caliber of the All Russia staff. Most were highly trained and knowledgeable about blindness as well as administration. He pointed out that every manager and assistant manager of the All Russia Association must attend a two-year training program at the Institute for Managers in Moscow to learn how to run a business as well as become sensitive to the needs of blind people.

Gallagher noted that Soviet rehabilitation professionals view the newly blinded individual's psychological and social adjustment to blindness as an important part of the rehabilitation process and that family members often participate in the training programs. They said that the effects of glasnost were apparent in the willingness of Soviet blindness professionals to talk about their problems and needs.

****

Rocks: The Blind Guy at the Lake

An unnamed classmate of Holy Cross commented concerning Rocks as follows: *The man had superb political instincts and knew how to operate, though he assured me that he was never a lobbyist for the blind. The lobbying was done by another organization that was competitive with his. One day, when he was at the peak of his powers directing the American Foundation for the Blind, he was coming to Boston to arrange a special event for a Helen Keller anniversary commemoration, and he wanted to know if I could set him up with an appointment to see Kevin White, then Mayor of Boston, in order to secure the best possible venue for his event. Rocks understood the importance of going to the top. He also understood that none of his classmates would ever say "no" to any request he made and he did not hesitate to ask. The meeting with Mayor White was arranged and Rocks set up his event just the way he wanted it.*

John Kelly recalls:

On the political side of things, Rocks was an ardent Democrat. His all time political hero was Robert F. Kennedy. He loved him because he always stood up for the little man and the down-trodden of our society. Bill was convinced that R.F.K. would one day make a great President. An assassin's bullet destroyed that dream.

****

The Migel Medal was established in 1937 by AFB's first president, M.C. Migel, to honor professionals and volunteers whose dedication and achievements have significantly improved the lives of blind and visually impaired people.

This award was presented to Donald H. Wedewer in 1990. He had served the State of Florida, Division of Blind Services for over 25 years. Wedewer was also instrumental in merging the American Association of Workers for the Blind and the Association for Education of the Visually Handicapped into the Association for Education and Rehabilitation of the Blind and Visually Impaired. He served as a member of the AFB's Board of Directors from 1982 and was still serving in this capacity when the Migel Medal was presented to him. Wedewer is an honored veteran of World War II, serving his nation with great distinction. During the War, he became blinded and a double leg amputee.

Wedewer first met Bill Gallagher when he was with the Pittsburgh Guild for the Blind. What Don admired most about Bill was his inspirational leadership of the AFB. On a social level, he described Bill as being "friendly, fun and always a gentleman."

A funny incident occurred in Fort Lauderdale, Florida. Bill flew down from New York to visit with Don and his wife and several other friends. He registered in the wrong hotel and no one showed up to be with him. The taxi driver had, by mistake, taken him to the wrong hotel. When they finally got together, the ever thoughtful Rocks told Don and his wife to be nice to the driver, who had made an honest mistake.

One evening, Don and his wife went to a local restaurant with Bill. Don said his wife fawned over a woman, who was standing at their table, as the three of them sat down. Mrs. Wedewer, thinking she was a guest, said to her, "how nice it was that she could come for their little gathering."

It turned out that the woman was not a guest, but rather the owner of the restaurant. Rocks and Don had a few chuckles over Mrs. Wedewer's faux pas.

****

EDITORIALS

While Bill Gallagher was the Executive Director of the AFB, he wrote a number of editorials for the AFB News reflecting his deep insight on the challenge confronting the blind community.

Some of his editorials are as follows:

PUBLIC EDUCATION DETER   DISCRIMINATION IN HIGH PLACES

In the ever-changing climate of Federal policy and initiatives, our greatest victories are often followed by resounding disappointments. For example, in the same year that the 100th Congress passed two comprehensive civil rights bills prohibiting discrimination against disabled people – the Fair Housing Act and the Civil Rights Restoration Act of 1988 – the U.S. Senate Department ruled that blind people are not suited to be United States diplomats. (My letter to the editor of the **New York Times** *about this ruling appears herein under the heading "DISCRIMINATION AT STATE").*

Why the double message, you might ask. For one, I think it reflects a weak link in our public education effort. Despite the fact that blind people do compete in the job market, governmental officials and the general public still harbor many misconceptions about what a blind person can or cannot do. Correcting these misconceptions is often an uphill battle. Nonetheless, it is a fight that the blindness field must pursue more aggressively.

At AFB, we provide public education through several mediums. To name a few – publications, public service announcements, and staff training and outreach to employers and corporations.

One of our most effective tools – and "secret weapons" – is the Job Index / User Network. This database lists over 1,200 blind and visually impaired people who use alternative techniques or technology to do their work successfully. It lists many careers previously thought "unthinkable" for blind people, including nursing, graphic arts, engineering and investment services. More than anything else, the Job Index / User Network offers proof positive that blind people can work in every major employment field.

Rocks: The Blind Guy at the Lake

Technology is, of course, one of the greatest employment equalizers of our time, offering a wide-range of talking products and computers with large-print, Braille and voice output. But we must also credit innovative rehabilitation practitioners, vocational counselors and other blindness professionals who help create alternative techniques and low-tech products that enable blind and visually impaired people to work side-by-side with their sighted peers.

With this, there is room for optimism. The current labor shortage in the allied health services field, for example, has opened new career paths to blind and visually impaired people in recent years. Other fields are sure to follow suit.

The ball is clearly in our court. Whether we write to protest State Department rulings or resistance in the private work sphere, it is the responsibility of the blindness field to let the secret out of the bag about the employability of blind people. I urge you all to rank public education about blindness and blind people among your top program priorities. This will undoubtedly score victories in the public and private sector.

****

LIVING IN THE INFORMATION AGE

We have a habit of naming decades for the significant events that occur during them. The 1960's for example, are recalled by many as the "Age of Aquarius" and the 1970's were labeled the "Me Decade." A fitting name for the 1980's, I think, would be the "Information Age."

Just look at what has happened during the past ten years. Computers have shrunk not only in size, but in price, and personal computers are fixtures in many American homes and offices. This trend has had a profound impact on the lives of blind and visually impaired people. For when equipped with Braille, large-print or voice output, these devices provide instant access to information.

Radio reading services have proven an effective way of

providing print-handicapped people with direct and convenient access to newspapers, magazines and books. The more than 100 radio reading services located throughout the country do an excellent job of keeping print-handicapped people up-to-date on current events by broadcasting news features, sports, editorials, business and advertisements. Many radio reading services broadcast 24-hours a day. However, scheduling does not always allow visually impaired people to hear all the news they would like when they would like to hear it.

In this issue of <u>AFB NEWS</u> you will read about technological advances that give blind and visually impaired people instant access to their local papers. AFB Southwest regional director July Scott is able to download the <u>Fort Worth Star-Telegram</u> onto her personal computer. A veteran radio announcer Jim Daugherty is piloting a "Talking Newspaper" in Michigan which allows visually impaired people to use their touch-tone telephones to select which articles they would like to hear.

Television is another major source of information for most Americans. When sighted people meet me for the first time, they are surprised to learn that I am as familiar with television programming as they are. I have found that by listening carefully I can generally get all the information I need about the program or commercial I am watching. A notable exception was a recent ad campaign by a car manufacturer. The spokesperson would make outrageous claims about his product while a caption underneath read "He's lying." Since I could not see the caption, I never got the joke and wondered how the manufacturer could afford to sell cars for only $100. Descriptive Video Services promises to open television to visually impaired viewers much as close-captioning did for people with hearing impairments.

AFB helps blind and visually impaired people, their families and friends, students and professionals to keep abreast of these developments in a myriad of ways. Our National Technology Center hosts a product demonstrations on a regular basis and the M.C. Migel Memorial Library and Information Center responds to

　　　　　Page 98

more than 250,000 information request annually. The AFB Publications Catalog lists dozens of textbooks, research papers, pamphlets, guides, manuals and general interest publications on all non-medical aspects of blindness and visual impairment. Through its exhibits program, AFB is able to bring information to a wide range of audiences – from school children visiting the United Nations headquarters in New York City to ophthalmologists attending a professional conference in New Orleans. And AFB's governmental relations department and regional centers alert their constituencies of developments in their areas through newsletters, bulletins and database services.

We are clearly living in an information age. The recent computerization of America has opened countless opportunities for blind and visually impaired people. It is up to us to see that blind and visually impaired people are not left out of the technological revolution that is sure to grow even more in the 1990's.

****

DISCRIMINATION AT STATE
To the Editor of <u>The New York Times</u>:

I read with concern that the State Department has ruled that blind people are not suited to be United States diplomats because they are unable to work with printed documents without resorting to Braille or sighted readers (news story, Nov. 29). State Department officials have not kept abreast of new technologies that enable the blind and visually impaired to work with materials in print.

For those with limited vision, there are closed-circuit television devices that provide magnification up to 60 times. A movable platform allows the user to scan printed materials.

Computerized reading machines, including the new Kurzwell personal reader, allows blind people to read typewritten or typeset print by converting it into easily understood synthetic speech. The personal reader is portable and can include a handheld scanner, a desktop scanner or both.

Synthetic speech computer software and large-print displays enable the blind and visually impaired to work with the same information as sighted co-workers. Hard copy is standard print, large print or Braille can be generated at the same time. Additional information may be had from the American Foundation for the Blind's National Technology Center, 15 West 16th Street, New York, New York 10011.

I'm sure there are legitimate reasons some people are not suited for diplomatic careers. But being blind isn't one of them.

Officials of government must realize their responsibility to end discrimination based on disability. The State Department's decision on the blind should be reversed immediately.

****

THE IMPORTANCE OF POSITIVE ROLE MODELS

The issue of what constitutes an appropriate and positive role model made headlines this spring when some students at Wellesley College objected to First Lady Barbara Bush as the featured speaker at their graduation ceremony. They argued that the First Lady's status in society was wholly dependent on her role as wife of the President and that a woman's college should only extend such an honor to a woman who has achieved success in her own right.

After reading numerous editorials pointing out the pros and cons of both sides of the debate I began to wonder about role models and how they're developed. In simplest terms a role model is a person whose behavior is imitated by others. People are drawn to different characteristics that they like and admire and the process is largely unconscious.

Looking back, I realize that literally dozens of people have had a significant impact on who I am today. These range, for instance, from my father, who had a tremendous work ethic, to a college roommate with a terrific sense of humor. And, being of Irish descent and coming out of Boston, I, of course, admired the Kennedys. While I had heard of Helen Keller, I did not actually meet another blind person until I enrolled at the Perkins School for the Blind. Talking to teachers, students, alumni and other visually impaired people who had gone to college and were working as professionals provided a tremendous boost to my self-esteem.

If they could do it, I thought, so could I. Prior to Perkins, however, I must admit that I was skeptical of my chances to earn a high school diploma, much less a master's degree.

I think that visually impaired students in mainstreamed settings today feel the same sense of isolation I did. Not only do they have little contact with other people with visual impairments, limited access to printed materials makes it difficult for them to even read about successful blind adults. In this issue of <u>AFB News</u> you will read about AFB's efforts to promote communication between visually impaired youngsters and adults. AFB-sponsored Braille readers at National Library Week read-a-thons in Atlanta, New York City and Washington, D.C., for example, gave blind and sighted children a chance to ask blind adults such pressing questions as "What is it like to be blind?," "Where do you work?" and "How do you read your mail?"

Many of these questions are also addressed in the new AFB book, <u>Career Perspectives: Interviews With Blind and Visually Impaired Professionals</u>, containing real-life stories from blind and visually impaired people who have succeeded in a wide range of "non-traditional" jobs. <u>Career Perspectives</u> was published, in part, to provide role models for blind and visually impaired students who are making career choices.

AFB's Careers and Technology Information Bank (CTIB) shows that blind and visually impaired people are working in a wide range of professional and managerial positions. However, few blind and visually impaired students are aware of the many career paths that are open to them. It is my hope that the personal accounts contained in Career Perspectives will inspire others to aspire to their highest hopes and dreams.

Also highlighted in this issue are profiles of consumers of blindness services who participated in the 1990 Helen Keller Seminar. They are all very different people who have, through their own accomplishments, changed people's attitudes about what a visually impaired person can or cannot do.

In researching the subject further, I found, surprisingly enough, that fame is seldom a consideration when developing role models. Indeed, the closer a person is to you, the more likely he or she is to become a role model. Encouraging direct contact between disabled youngsters and adults is the driving force behind the Harold Russell Motivational Institute, Inc. (HRMI). I am pleased to serve on the board of directors of this non-profit organization which aims to increase education, employment and career advancement opportunities for people with disabilities by developing a network of successfully employed disabled persons who are willing to serve as role models/peer advisors for others.

As for Barbara Bush being an appropriate and positive role model, I think she fits the bill on all counts. I am especially impressed by the way she was able to galvanize the entire nation behind the cause of literacy – another topic covered in this newsletter. She has set a fine example for others to follow and that's what role models are all about.

****

WE MUST SPEAK UP FOR SERVICES IN THESE FISCALLY – PRUDENT TIMES

NEW YORK – These are times of diminishing expectations and hard choices. As we enter 1991, we face sobering realities – recessions, a war in another part of the world, and the erosion of services in our big cities and states.

Rocks: The Blind Guy at the Lake

Where does that leave the state or services for blind and visually impaired Americans? I am no soothersyer, but I do believe that along with so many other social services in jeopardy in this gloomy economic climate, programs serving the needs of blind and visually impaired persons will be put through the litmus test as never before. How well these programs fare in the mine fields of the budgetary process will depend on what we - professionals, parents, and blind and visually impaired persons - are willing to do to defend these services. What I am talking about here is advocacy.

As a footnote, I offer you this story from the December 18, 1990 edition of the <u>New York Times</u>. The article states that when officials from Gallaudet University, the only institution of higher learning in the country for deaf persons, went to Capitol Hill in 1989 for more federal money, members of both Houses of Congress told them they had not asked for enough money. The reporter suggests that the unexpected increase may have been linked to the national attention that was generated by earlier advocacy efforts of the student body to elect its first deaf college president.

This story provides us with an object lesson about the power of advocacy. Whether we write letters to our Congressional representatives or send editorials to our newspapers, we who have a stake in services for blind and visually impaired persons must stick our collective necks out and speak up. As federal and state cost-saving measures pare away at existing programs, we will no longer have the luxury of taking a "wait and see" attitude.

The staff of AFB's Washington, D.C.-based governmental relations department know this all too well. When federal offices shut down in the wake of the budget crisis of late October 1990, they spent many hours "on the Hill" educating Congressional staff about the needs of blind and visually impaired persons and the programs that must continue to meet those needs.

In this issue of <u>AFB NEWS</u>, you can read about another type of advocacy – the behind-the-scenes work representing the needs of *blind and visually impaired persons on a national committee charged with developing standards of accessibility for disabled people in public buildings and facilities. And as part of the AFB NEWS role model series, we feature a journalist who is blind who uses the power of the pen to advocate for the needs and perspectives of people with disabilities.*

In other highlights, the Winter 1991 AFB NEWS features contributions from the December 1990 special issue of the Journal of Visual Impairment & Blindness on the present and future direction of adaptive technology; a new publication about low vision eye conditions for those who want non-clinical, jargon-free explanations, and two national projects, one to develop curriculum training materials for teachers of deaf-blind children, and the other to develop a model for establishing low interest loans for adaptive technology for blind and visually impaired persons.

****

ACCESS TO SERVICES IS CAUSE FOR CONCERN FOR BLIND AND VISUALLY IMPAIRED PEOPLE

Remember the adage, "The more things change, the more they remain the same?" I think this maxim was coined by someone familiar with the blindness field – a consumer or parent, perhaps, who has gone through the process of obtaining education or rehabilitation services.

When I became blind in 1938 my parents didn't know what kind of services I'd need or how to go about getting them. And my doctors were able to offer them little more than medical advice. It is hard for me to believe now that we lived fewer than 20 miles from the Perkins Institute for the Blind, as it was known then, and knew nothing about it.

About three months after I lost my sight, my parents received a visit from someone from the Department of Education in Boston who asked if they wanted to send me to the Perkins Institution for the Blind. This person did not explain that Perkins was a school for blind and visually impaired children and that I would be able to earn my high school diploma there. My parents rejected the suggestion immediately. The word institution, I think, was too strong for them to deal with at the time.

I remained at home for the next three years wondering what my future was going to be. The little rehabilitation training I received during that time was provided by my friends, family and former classmates. Although amateurs at blindness rehabilitation, we learned together through trial and error and their efforts were effective. I knew nothing of the Talking Book program. Nor did I know the appropriate method of traveling with a sighted guide. And lessons in Braille were out of the question. The words "blind" and "Braille" were never uttered in the house while we still held out the hope that my sight would return as suddenly as it had disappeared.

Then in1941, my parents received another visit – this time from a representative of the Massachusetts Commission for the Blind who painted a positive picture of Perkins. I enrolled shortly thereafter. Back then there were no orientation and mobility specialists or rehabilitation teachers on the staff at Perkins because those professions did not exist.

My teachers taught me how to type and to read and write Braille. I learned independent travel and other daily living skills from my blind classmates. Most important, I think, the students and professional staff at Perkins provided me with the guidance and support I needed to come to terms with my blindness. It is unfortunate that this type of informal counseling was not available to my family as well.

Luckily, some things have changed drastically since then. For one, there are no more "institutions" for the blind. Indeed, there is no longer a homogenous population collectively known as "the blind." Services for blind and visually impaired people have been expanded and many are targeted to very specific groups such as preschoolers, people with multiple disabilities, working age visually impaired people, and nursing home residents, just to name a few.

Despite excellent progress, much work remains to be done in accessing better services for visually impaired people. We know from the calls and letters we receive that many visually impaired people still do not know what is available to them. For example, the mother of a visually impaired child called to say that she had heard of an "excellent" school for the blind in Pennsylvania and asked if AFB could provide her with the name of the school as well as enrollment information. Another caller wanted to know how he could join the Talking Books program.

In this issue of <u>AFB NEWS</u>, we identify and address some of the pressing concerns regarding the current state of services for blind and visually impaired people. You will read, for example, about new programs to train hospital staff about the unique needs for blind and visually impaired patients, and field visits to help other agencies evaluate and improve existing services. And you will read about efforts to educate and involve family members of blind and visually impaired people in evaluating and accessing services.

I am especially pleased that greater efforts are being made to include the entire family in the rehabilitation process. It is an idea whose time has come and I hope that this trend continues.

By focusing on these issues in <u>AFB NEWS</u>, we hope to inspire thoughts and ideas for action from our readers. We have come a long way in 50 years, but much work lies ahead.

****

THE NEED FOR ALL OF US TO HELP
EDUCATE THE PUBLIC ABOUT BLINDNESS

As a blind person, I sometimes wonder why sighted people are uneasy when they meet me for the first time. Later, after they become comfortable with me and other blind and visually impaired people, many sighted people often confess that they felt very nervous at the first meeting. Why?

Some sighted people claim that they simply did not know what to say or how to act. They were not quite sure about how to walk or eat with the blind person, and they were afraid they would say something to embarrass the blind individual.

They avoided the use of such words as blind, see and look. Or they purposely avoided an encounter with a blind person altogether. This, then, totally eliminated the possibility of saying or doing something embarrassing.

I have heard these same sighted people say later that if they had only known then what they know now about blindness and blind people, they would not have been frightened or uneasy.

I keep wondering what we in the blindness fields have done to cause this. Have our agencies done enough to educate the public about blindness? In our public education programs, do we present blind people in a realistic manner?

Part of the problem, I think, is that we do not stress enough that blind people are individuals – who happen to be blind.

It is the job of the professionals in the blindness field to educate the public about blindness and blind people.

We must be sensitive to the public's needs and misconceptions and provide the facts about blindness and blind people in a positive and realistic light.

When the general public feels comfortable with blind people as individuals, it will open many doors for all visually impaired people – on the job, at school, and in the everyday encounters.

I also feel that blind people can play a greater role in helping to put sighted people at ease.

Consider, for example, this scene: A blind person is hosting a business lunch at a restaurant. The waiter asks the blind person's companion, "What will he have?" The sighted person replies in a hostile tone, "Why don't you ask him?" And the blind person proclaims aloud, "I may not see but I'm not deaf."

I have witnessed this uncomfortable scene on many different occasions.

A better response on the part of that blind restaurant patron would be simply to turn and talk directly to the waiter. Nine times out of ten, the waiter will then talk directly to the blind customer while taking the rest of the order.

I feel the waiter cannot be blamed. He may not have encountered other blind people at the restaurant and, consequently may not know what to do, or not to do, when he meets a blind individual, or any disabled person.

Once I had lunch in my office with a gentleman who did not have any arms. I knew how I was going to handle my lunch but I had all kinds of questions as to how he was going to manage. After thinking about it for a while, I did what I like people to do for me. I asked him what assistance he needed and left it up to him to let me know. He said he would tell me how I could help, and from that point on, we had a pleasant lunch.

I'd be interested in hearing about your experiences and thoughts about how professionals in the blindness field as well as blind people themselves might do a better job in educating the public about blindness. Please drop me a line in care of AFB NEWS.

****

ACCESSIBILITY FOR DISABLED AMERICANS CAN BE A PERSONAL AND PROFESSIONAL COMMITMENT

Access is defined by Webster's Dictionary as "permission, liberty or ability to enter, approach, communicate with or pass to and from." Indeed, access for some 35 million disabled Americans can mean anything from getting into a building, to getting information, to getting a job and decent housing. And it is the rallying cry of a broad spectrum of organizations of and for people with disabilities.

In making presentations and speeches throughout the country, I have observed a greater awareness of this issue among professionals in disability-related and other fields. But I do question the extent to which sensitivity about accessibility concerns governs the way we think and conduct our professional and private lives.

In our own communities, for example, how many of us question the accessibility of our schools, libraries, churches and synagogues? And when planning conferences, how many of us scout the hotel or convention center to ensure that it is barrier-free, that all participants will be able to move around easily and safely, and that the sound system and lighting is adequate for people with hearing and vision problems, respectively?

Fortunately, there are individuals and organizations who have taken positive steps in ensuring accessibility for disabled people. In this issue of AFB NEWS, two such individuals are featured – Ann Corn, Ed.D., and Karen Luxton, Ed.D., both members of AFB's Journal of Visual Impairment & Blindness editorial advisory board. They have both worked to help eliminate physical and attitudinal barriers to religious worship for disabled people in their church and synagogue. Their suggestions for making a religious institution accessible are applicable for a wide range of business and community settings.

The Coalition for Information Access for Print Handicapped Readers, which is also featured in this issue, is working to make information more accessible for blind and visually impaired people. Chaired by Kathleen M. Huebner, Ph.D., Director of AFB's national services in education, low vision, and orientation and mobility, this exciting new network of blindness organizations had met several times this past year to coordinate strategies for making materials in Braille, large print and recorded formats more widely available for visually impaired people.

This concern about access to information has become a focal point of discussion for educators and blindness professionals who are witnessing growing numbers of blind people who are illiterate. In fact, in a historic meeting of blindness service providers and blind consumer groups in March 1989 in Baltimore, seven organizations – the Ad Hoc Committee on Joint Organizational Effort – drafted a consensus statement identifying access to information and illiteracy as a priority concern for both service providers and blind and visually impaired consumers. You can read more about this meeting in this newsletter.

As program chairperson for the 1990 annual meeting of the President's Committee on Employment of People with Disabilities (PCEPD), I have witnessed firsthand the efforts of another organization that has integrated accessibility concerns into its own policies. PCEPD Chairman Harold Russell cancelled the organization's 1991 meeting in San Antonio, Texas, when he discovered that the City's transit system does not equip a single bus with a wheelchair lift. Moreover, the City has no plans to purchase any in the future.

San Antonio's mass transit policy will end up costing the City at least $1.6 Million in lost revenue. A drastic decision you might think. But not when you consider that next to attitudinal barriers, transportation may be one of the most important barriers to employment of people with disabilities.

Instead, PCEPD has chosen a site which reflects the agency's goals and commitment to promoting employment for disabled people. The meeting will be held in Dallas, a City which plans to have its entire fleet of buses equipped with wheelchair lifts in the next five to eight years.

The efforts of individuals like Dr. Corn and Dr. Luxton must be encouraged, and so, too, must we support the efforts of organizations like PCEPD and the Ad Hoc Committee on Joint Organizational Effort. They have set an example for all of us to follow.

Page 110

Rocks: The Blind Guy at the Lake

AMERICANS WITH DISABILITIES ACT DESERVES OUR SUPPORT

Job discrimination is a violation of federal law, right? Consider the following situation:

A recent law school graduate, who is blind, is excited about the promise of his new career. He worked hard and graduated at the top of his class. He is also proud of the fact that he has managed to cover most of his college expenses with the help of some tuition assistance from his state rehabilitation agency and student loans.

This law school graduate has never been part of a disability rights movement or a member of a consumer organization of blind people. After all, he did not need all of that! He had made it on his own. Or, so he thought, until he started looking for a job.

After numerous job interviews, he discovered that many potential employers believed that he could not practice law because of his blindness. They suggested that he consider a career in estate planning where the reading load might not be so great. None called back for a second interview.

Unfortunately, for this blind individual and over 35 million disabled Americans, handicapped people are not covered by most of the Civil Rights Laws which protect other minority groups. Although Section 504 of the Rehabilitation Act of 1973 as amended does provide certain protections against discrimination on the basis of a handicap, Section 504 applies only to recipients of federal funds and does not protect against discrimination in the private sector.

Unless our law school graduate was protected against discrimination under state law, he would have no recourse against a private employer who either failed to hire or failed to promote a person because he or she was disabled.

There is promising new legislation, however, that would reverse this trend. Through identical bills introduced as Senate Bill S. 2345 by Senator Lowell Weicker (R-CT) and as House Bill H.R. 4498 by Representative Tony Coelho (D-CA), the Americans with Disabilities Act would be the first federal civil rights law benefiting handicapped people in the private sector.

The Americans with Disabilities Act covers employment, housing, public accommodations, transportation and communications access. It defines specifically what discrimination is, including various types of intentional and unintentional exclusion; inferior or less effective services, benefits or activities, and discriminatory qualifications and performance standards.

It also specifies actions that do not constitute discrimination such as treatment unrelated to a disability or the application of qualifications and performance standards necessary to doing a specific job.

The law's provisions include the concept of "reasonable accommodation," call for an issuance of minimum accessibility guidelines from the Architectural and Transportation Barriers Compliance Board and provides administrative and judicial remedies for violations of the law.

AFB supports the Americans with Disabilities Act and urges its prompt enactment into law.

For further details about this law and how you can support it, write or call Scott Marshall, AFB Governmental Relations Specialist, American Foundation for the Blind, 1615 M St. NW, Suite 250, Washington, D.C. 10036; (202) 457-1487.

****

LET'S TAKE BLINDNESS OUT OF THE DARK

As Executive Director of a national blindness organization, I make it my business – and the business of the entire agency – to dispel negative stereotypes and myths about blind people. Indeed, in this column, I have urged professionals in the blindness field, to be sensitive to the public's needs and misconceptions about what a blind person can or cannot do.

So, I am especially concerned about the way in which blindness agencies depict blindness. Do we portray blind people in a positive and realistic light? Do we provide accurate descriptions of blindness in our public education campaigns?

Generally, I think we have all done, and are doing, a good job in showing that blind and visually impaired people lead meaningful and productive lives.

In some instances, however, we fall short of that goal. I am referring specifically to fund-raising materials that promote the idea that blind people live in a world of darkness.

"Contribute to our agency," the appeal letters cry out, "and take a blind person out of the dark."

I have a problem with this type of appeal for two reasons – it perpetuates a common and popular misconception, and the language of the appeal connotes negative associations.

First, the misconception. We know that blindness is not darkness, but the absence of sight. The fact is most people classified as blind, have varying degrees of vision - only a small percentage are totally blind. Also, adventitiously, blind people who once experienced sight, retain a visual memory of objects and people. They can visualize the red truck or the green tree.

Congenitally, totally blind people cannot visualize colors or objects like sighted or adventitiously blind people, because they have not had the visual experience.

And what about negative associations? Many sighted people associate the idea of darkness with a feeling of helplessness, a vulnerability to the hidden, scary things that go bump in the night. Children, imagining monsters and ghosts, are usually afraid to sleep without the lights on. Adults are nervous about walking into a dark house or room.

The image of the helpless blind person living in darkness, is also not that different from an older, and unfortunately, still existent negative stereotype of blind people personified as street corner beggars peddling pencils.

This tear-jerker type of appeal, not only promotes an inaccurate depiction of blindness, but also fuels people's worst fears and sentiments.

We must, therefore, very carefully consider our approach to the general public in seeking their support of our programs.
■■■

****

NEWS ITEMS OF INTEREST FROM THE "AFB NEWS"

Following are some excerpts and articles from the <u>AFB NEWS</u>, relative to Gallagher's tenure at the AFB and some of the awards presented to him for contributions that he made to the blind community:

GALLAGHER HONORED FOR OUTSTANDING CONTRIBUTIONS TO DISABILITY ORGANIZATIONS

AFB President and Executive Director William F. Gallagher was recently named recipient for three awards, honoring outstanding contributions to organizations of and for disabled people.

The setting was Princeton, New Jersey, on April 20, when Gallagher received the Evelyn Aronow Dolan Memorial Award presented by the New Jersey Commission on Recreation for the Handicapped. This award, the most prestigious bestowed by the Commission, is given to an individual who has promoted the growth and development of community recreation services for disabled people in New Jersey. The award was presented, in part, for Gallagher's efforts to make museum and art gallery collections accessible to blind and visually impaired people (see AFB NEWS, January–April 1990).

Also honoring Gallagher was the Association of Radio Reading Services which presented him with its C. Stanley Porter Award at the Association's annual convention on May 27 in San Francisco. Radio reading services are special radio stations that make information from newspapers, books and magazines available to blind and other print handicapped people by reading it over the airwaves. The Porter Award recognizes Gallagher's contributions through the years to the Association's goal of enabling print handicapped people to keep abreast of current events and to live independently and knowledgeably.

Finally, on June 20 at Williamsburg, Virginia, the American Association of the Deaf-Blind (AADB) presented Gallagher with its Peter J. Salmon Award which honors professionals in the disability field who have made outstanding contributions to the deaf-blind population. Said Roderick J. MacDonald, AADB President, "We salute Bill Gallagher's long and dedicated service to blind and deaf-blind individuals and his leadership in supporting the national organization of deaf-blind people."

During the early part his career, Gallagher, blind since the age of 15, focused on the special rehabilitation needs of newly blinded adults. Among his accomplishments, he spearheaded and established innovative rehabilitation programs in Boston, Pittsburgh and New York City. Gallagher joined AFB in 1972 as director of program planning and was named associate director for advocacy in 1978. Two years later he was appointed Executive Director.

****

GALLAGHER RECEIVES OPTOMETRY AWARD

DENVER – AFB Executive Director William F. Gallagher

was awarded the 1987 Carel C. Koch Memorial Medal, a top honor in the optometry community, at a ceremony held there on December 6.

Presented by the American Academy of Optometry, the award is given annually in recognition of outstanding contributions to the enhancement and development of relations between optometry and other professions.

"We applaud the dedication and commitment of Mr. Gallagher and his staff in strengthening relations between optometrists and professionals in the blindness field," said Dr. Richard L. Hopping, Chief of the American Academy of Optometry Awards Committee and President of the Southern California College of Optometry.

In presentation remarks made during the Academy's annual meeting, Dr. Hopping cited AFB's leadership in promoting low vision services through seminars and publications, developing guidelines and standards for low vision facilities, agencies and professionals, and inclusion of optometrists and ophthalmologists in its programs and on advisory committees.

"It is truly an honor to receive this prestigious award," Gallagher said. "The American Academy of Optometry has maintained high standards in the areas of research and education, ensuring the delivery of quality low vision services to thousands of visually impaired people nationwide. It is with great appreciation for the Academy's efforts that I accept this award."

Fay Hava Jarosh in her article encapsulates one of Gallagher's greatest attributes in managing the affairs of the AFB:

Rallying for teamwork is an ongoing cause of William G. Gallagher, executive director of the American Foundation for the Blind (AFB).

For, he said, it is teamwork which has enabled AFB to forge a partnership with over 1,000 specialized schools, agencies and organizations offering services to blind and visually impaired people nationwide.

And it is teamwork which has empowered the working mandate of AFB since its founding in 1921: to advocate, develop and provide programs and services to help blind and visually impaired people achieve independence with dignity in all sectors of society.

Gallagher attributes the growth of these services and programs to the hard work and commitment of individuals such as Helen Keller and other pioneers in the blindness field. As AFB's counselor on national and international relations from 1924 until her death in 1968, Keller traveled across the country to educate legislators and the public about the needs of blind people.

Gallagher is proud of the accomplishments that have marked AFB's efforts to continue Helen Keller's work – thanks to the continued support of donors, the people who benefit from AFB's services, the cooperation of professionals in the blindness and low vision fields, and the hard work and dedication of AFB's staff, board of trustees and other volunteers.

"It is this kind of teamwork," Gallagher said, "which reinforces our commitment to the demands of the present and the challenges of the suture."

And one of AFB's most exciting challenges, according to Gallagher, is technology – putting it to work to help meet the independent living needs of blind and visually impaired people.

****

SPUNGIN TRIBUTE TO WILLIAM F. GALLAGHER

Susan J. Spungin is the Vice President of Education and International Programs at the AFB. In February 1991, William F. Gallagher received an Access Award at the Josephine L. Taylor Leadership Institute.

On that occasion, Ms. Spungin gave the following tribute to Gallagher:

"If we see further than our predecessors, it's because we stand on the shoulders of giants." *That quote certainly applies directly to me personally, and I am sure many others who have witnessed Bill's achievements over the years, especially his ability to open doors, symbolically and in actuality, to provide blind and visually impaired individuals with life opportunities and access to self-determination.*

"Giants are not made without the influence of past giants' shoulders on which they stood." *In this instance, the man we honor, had a mentor in his life of major proportions, both physically and mentally. The giant of the past for this person was Father Carroll, a man of commitment, of insight, of thirst for understanding of the human condition and a man, in his time, of great controversy. These qualities certainly have influenced the recipient of this award, William F. Gallagher. Having worked with Bill Gallagher for the past 19 years, I have had the opportunity to learn the true meaning of the concept of commitment – commitment not only to the issue of equality and rights for blind and visually impaired individuals, but also commitment to his belief in the basic goodness in all individuals, regardless of how others might view them.*

Bill often attempts the impossible and to the amazement of many, often succeeds. I personally can attest to that when looking at AFB in 1972 and comparing it to now in 1991. Under Bill's leadership, AFB has professionalized and centered its mission to the needs of blind and visually impaired people, as never was done previously. He organized, for the first time in 1982, a Board/Staff Seminar that no one thought possible. He has masterfully developed AFB's Board to better represent the field of blindness, and has convinced the lay members of the Board, that professional comment is, at the very least, as important as that of the business person.

I could go on and on, but let me end with Bill's willingness to take on controversial issues – namely, his dream, and potentially now, a reality, that the field come together to include all constituencies, especially those groups represented by the affiliated consumers. Regardless of the controversy, Bill has, over the past 10 years, again attempted the imagined impossible, that being, bringing the blindness field together, including all blindness consumer groups. If someone had told me in 1975 that AFB would be sitting around a table with AER and all the consumer groups, I would have passed out in disbelief.

Think what you will of the outcome; the fact is the field is talking together – accessing, if you will, face to face – input from constituencies never before thought possible.

In conclusion, a tribute to Bill Gallagher's leadership can easily be seen in the context of access.

He has enabled access to information by his commitment to technology and the development of the National Technology Center at AFB, as well as his vision and support to audio description and talking newspapers.

He has facilitated access to the environment in terms of his belief and support for access to cultural institutions, as well as culturally appropriate materials, not to mention the renovation plans for AFB's national office in New York.

He has fostered better access to services through his commitment to professionalism and advocacy. So, Bill, all I can say and I am sure I represent everyone who has worked with you over the years, is that we thank you for allowing us to access you, which has enriched our lives and the lives of blind and visually impaired people throughout the world.

Rocks: The Blind Guy at the Lake

I will lead the blind on their journey; by paths unknown-known I will guide them. I will turn darkness into light before them, and make crooked ways straight. These things I do for them, and I will not forsake them. (Isaia, 42-16)

BILL GALLAGHER ON BLINDNESS

In 1990, Bill Gallagher presented a paper at the National Convention of the National Rehabilitation Association in Detroit, Michigan, entitled: "A Blind Person Reviews Blindness in 1990."

This paper offers deep insight on the problems which confronted blind people in the 1950's and 1960s, in their attempt to become fully integrated in our society. Bill's analysis and review shows how far Father Carroll's dreams have come true. There is yet much to be done.

Bill Gallagher's paper follows in its entirety:

A Blind Person Reviews Blindness in 1990

As a blind person, a question that I have been asked many times is: "Is it worse to be born blind or to lose your sight as an adult?" "Is it better to have seen and lost your sight than never to have seen at all?" This is a topic that is discussed frequently in 1990. Does the individual who has been blind since birth, or the individual who has lost his sight as an adult, have more problems in adjusting to life. As a blind person, I do not know the answer, but I have given it a great deal of thought. I imagine that it will be discussed for many years to come. But I do know that in 1990, agencies make a distinction between the problems of a blind person and those of a blinded person. As I look back in history, let us say to the early 60's, it must have been very confusing for a blind person to be classified and categorized in the same group with people who had lost their sight as adults. We now know that both groups need help but that they have separate and distinct problems. For example: the problems of a married man, twenty-five years old, with two children, who loses his sight at the age of twenty-four, are all together different than those of the twenty-five year old blind man who seems to be having trouble adjusting to life. The fifty-nine year old recently blinded grandmother has different problems than the twenty-nine year old blind woman who is seeking employment. I feel today, 1990, that blindness is still a severe and tragic blow to a person – it shatters his total personality organization – but that a blind person of today has many more advantages than those at the mid-century mark.

It's a wonderful feeling to know that blindness is not darkness but the absence of light. How misleading it must have been to the general public when agencies and other so-called responsible people referred to blind people as living in the world of the dark. How confusing it must have been to a person who was approaching the problem of blindness when all he knew was that he was going to live for the rest of his life in darkness. No wonder there was a wall built up between sighted people and those without sight. Just imagine, in the early 60's, the legal definition of blindness was: "A person shall be considered blind whose central acuity does not exceed 20/200 in the better eye with correcting lenses." In those days, people with some vision were classified as blind. What a horrible position in which to place a partially sighted person. I wonder what this must have done to his self-image? I wonder what this did to the totally blind person in those days? How confused the general public must have been when they saw a so-called blind person doing things with his sight. Some people in the early 60's held conferences to come up with a more realistic definition of blindness. A definition that would be beneficial to the blind person and also satisfactory to the person whose vision was impaired. It wasn't until the early 1970's that the more realistic and fair definition of blindness was established. We now have agencies working with blind people and other agencies working with individuals with impaired vision, but their offices are not under the same roof.

In 1990, we do not find duplication of services in the same city or area. This was always a problem not only to the agencies but was also extremely upsetting to the blind person. It led to blind persons being shuffled from place to place without any direction or plans for future goals. By the way, agencies began to recognize this problem in the mid-60's, but because of tradition, fund-raising purposes, and a "set-in-their-ways" board, agencies were unable to do much about it. It wasn't until they established a certification board handled by a national organization that duplications of services were eliminated. Agencies that have been certified give a more professional and complete service to blind people. At this time, a blind person does not have to live down or live with, the emotional jargon that was fed to the general public in the past during fund-raising time. Some well-known slogans popular in the early 60's were: "Give to the people who live in the dark so that they may live in the light;" "Help this depressed helpless blind man;" "Give to the sightless so that they may be happy'" and one that did as much harm, "Let our blind do your nuisance jobs, we have cheap labor in our sheltered shops." Blind people of today have a much better chance to compete with their fellow man because the agencies give a more accurate and fair description of blindness to the general public. The sighted people do not seem to be as tense and nervous now when they meet a blind person as they were in the past. They have a more wholesome and realistic attitude towards blindness. They see the fellow blind man as an individual, one who has interests due to his nature and personality and not due to his blindness.

The general public seems to have a better knowledge of blindness, therefore, parents of blind children see a brighter future for their child. They are still shocked and disturbed when the pediatrician tells them that their child is blind. They are loaded with emotional feelings. The pediatrician and the ophthalmologist of today now recognize and appreciate rehabilitation, therefore, they are able to discuss with parents the advantages of professional social service assistance. Today parents receive this assistance shortly after the birth of the blind child and are unable to hinder the child's emotional and educational growth. Parents have a better understanding of what blindness is and what they may expect for this child, and therefore, blindness does not interfere with inter-personal relationships within the family group.

Training in orientation starts in the baby's crib. In these early days, how important it is to work with the child to train his senses to the optimum and to assist this youngster so that he may be in contact with his environment. There are lessons to help this child during his creeping and crawling stages and special exercises for him so that he may look natural in his physical movements. Professional counseling and reassurance is given to the parents while the child is going through the weaning stage. What a depressing sight it must have been years ago for the blind child and his family when he had to leave home at the age of six to enter a residential school for the blind many miles away. I wonder if we will ever know how much this affected the child, how much this interfered with his emotional growth.

Yes, today we still have residential schools for the blind children, but they are only for those with multiple handicaps or children who are unable to compete with sighted children in the school systems in their respective towns. Four major problems: communications, mobility, educating the school system, and handling the parent's feelings about their child competing with sighted children, have been overcome, and the blind child has now taken his place with his sighted classmates. The trend towards integrating the blind child into local school systems started in the early 50's. It was a slow process but a very fruitful one.

The blind child of today has the necessary skills and tools to allow him to be in positive competition with other children. A study made in the early 60's showed that a blind child could read 90 words a minute in Braille while a sighted child could read print at 250 words a minute. This shows, in just the communications field, how much a blind child was handicapped in those days. Today, due to modern equipment, a portable machine that translates the printed word, such as textbooks, daily and weekly newspapers, comic books, popular magazines, the "John Glenn Missile Series," into sound, and the other devices that enable the blind child to write print; the blind child can compete with the sighted child in the same school.

The blind child now has the privilege of traveling independently with the use of the electronic mobile unit. The child does not have to depend upon older brothers and sisters, taxis, or classmates to escort him to and from school. He is able to make a freedom of choice whenever he wants to move. This has broadened the child's acquaintances. This has enabled him to play a more important part during recess and after school hours. Because of equal opportunities with communications and mobility, the child has the opportunity to develop adequate and proper techniques of daily living. Today, the schools no longer have the fear of accepting the blind child; the teacher no longer has the anxiety of how to reach and educate this child; the parents are no longer frightened and tormented as they see the child leave for school in the morning; the sighted classmate no longer sees the blind child as a freak but he learns about blindness as he grows up and competes with his fellow classmate who happens to be blind; but most of all, the blind child has the opportunity of the give and take which is so important in the emotional growth of a youngster. The blind child has the opportunity to develop his personality to its optimum.

And now in the school systems, the social workers have merged with the educators and we have the Social-Educational Department. This So-Ed Department plays a major function in the academic school system. Through proper guidance and counseling, the child is able to pick his own field according to his natural ability, interest, and capacity. We see blind people today in many professional and business fields that were unheard of at the mid-century mark. But people in those days were beginning to think of professional jobs for blind people. We saw a start of people breaking into many occupations when the war blinded returned home after the Second World War. We saw some, but, oh so few, blind persons going into the legal, educational and other professional fields. They were the real pioneers in opening new opportunities for us in 1990. They deserve a great deal of credit because if it were not for some courageous blind persons in those days and for advanced, thinking, workers, we today would not have the privilege and choice of picking our vocations, and, yes, even avocations. People who are blind owe a great deal to those who broke the blind barrier. And we saw in the early 60's books being written about professional jobs for blind people – PROFESSIONAL JOBS FOR BLIND PERSONS, co-author, Norman Yoder, Ph.D. In those days, the professional blind person would hit headlines, today he is just another business man with a job to do.

During the Second World War, workers gave some thought to rehabilitation for the blinded person. Statistics were showing that over 85% of the blind population had lost their sight as adults, therefore, the urgent need for rehabilitation. People began to realize that a person lost more than just his sight when he became blind. Experts in the field started to analyze blindness. Conferences were held bringing experts together to study rehabilitation and rehabilitation centers. A new book was published in the early 60's in which the author, Rev. Thomas J. Carroll, analyzed blindness. The book was advanced for its time but now plays a very important part in every agency's philosophy, federal or private, in work with blind people. Today, we no longer see sheltered shops that isolated blind persons from the employment market; instead we see regional rehabilitation centers which enable a blinded adult to reach his own total rehabilitation. It assists the blinded person with his problems brought on because of blindness and these centers help to restore or find a realistic substitute for the things the individual has lost because of blindness. But most of all it gives the individual the opportunity of returning to the sighted community and re-establishing himself in the family, in his career, and in his social activities.

Blindness is no longer synonymous with poverty. The streets have been cleared of blind beggars who are so harmful to the public's concept of blindness. Today, rehabilitation is not just for the poor and the extremely rich, but it is for all individuals who need the service. We now no longer have an economics needs test to determine who is eligible for rehabilitation services. As I mentioned previously, blindness no longer means poverty because the Federal Government and its wonderful and important Social Insurance Act, which was passed in 1967, entitled the blinded adult to an adequate income. This came under the revision of the old Social Security Act.

Today, the aged blind person is not being forgotten. Agencies have a team of techniques instructors, peripathologists, and psycho-social workers reaching the aged so that they may lead more active and useful lives as retired persons. The elderly person is no longer in a rocking chair sitting out the rest of his life but remains an active person in the community. Who knows, but before 1995, we may have blind people driving rockets from one city to another and shortly after the turn of the century, we may have instruments which will help a blind person to see without the use of his eyes.

Blind persons have many people to thank for their status in the community today: all of the scientists who worked on the missile projects during the space age for their contributions to sensory training and the instruments that now help a blind person with his mobility orientation and communication; the professional workers who were pioneers in starting programs and projects so that a blind person is now independent and recognized as an individual; the blind persons who had the courage and stamina to further their education; and all those who helped to develop new openings in the labor market. All of these people have contributed to the forward movement, so that now, we who are blind in 1990, are able to take our rightful places in a sighted society. Yes, and even Father Carroll has another new book out, <u>BLINDNESS, WHAT IT IS, WHAT IT DOES, AND I'M GLAD PEOPLE ARE DOING SOMETHING ABOUT IT</u>.

Gallaher's essay reminded Thomas Costello, a civil trial lawyer, of a memorable incident in a courtroom. Costello recalls, "After the jury was selected in walked the judge with the assistance of a blind man's cane. I could not believe my eyes: how could a blind man conduct a trial? Documents were offered into evidence, and objections were made to those documents, causing the judge to have to examine them. But the judge had an easy answer to the problem. He would declare a brief recess and go to his chambers and have his secretary go over the written or typed material with him. The judge handled the trial with great ease and experience, just as well as any sighted judge I had ever appeared before."

****

GALLAGHER TO RETIRE FROM AFB IN 1991

NEW YORK – William F. Gallagher has announced that he will retire in 1991 as President and Executive Director of AFB, ending his more than 40-year tenure in the blindness field.

Gallagher said he has chosen to retire at a time when AFB is involved in identifying critical issues for the 1990's and beyond. "With the passage of the Americans with Disabilities Act, the Foundation is at the brink of new and exciting challenges," said Gallagher. "I want to make sure that AFB can provide continued leadership through the 1990's and that my successor has the opportunity to be involved in designing strategies for those challenges and for the future."

Among the challenges, Gallagher cited AFB's plans to play a leadership role in ensuring that blind and visually impaired people benefit from the choices that the Americans with Disabilities Act legislated and assisting the larger community in making these options readily available. This includes, for example, making employment, public transportation, and all other aspects of community life, such as museums, fully accessible to blind and visually impaired people.

Gallagher noted that blind and visually impaired people have many more options today than they had when he became blind nearly 50 years ago. "New adaptive technologies have opened up a wide spectrum of new opportunities for blind and visually impaired people at home, school, in the workplace and in their communities."

Over the next several months, Gallagher will be working closely with the AFB Board of Trustees and staff involved in the Foundation's strategic planning process. "I am committed to a smooth transition to ensure that AFB fulfills its responsibilities as the leading national organization in the blindness field."

A search committee chaired by Michael M. Maney, partner in the law firm of Sullivan & Cromwell and Chairman of the Executive Committee of AFB's Board, has been formed to seek Gallagher's successor.

****

WILLIAM GALLAGHER'S FAREWELL

There is a time in everyone's life when they start to think of retiring. For me, that time came in the last few years. I decided to retire in the spring of 1991, and to return to my home state, Massachusetts. I announced my decision to retire at an AFB Board of Trustees Meeting in the spring of 1990, and after much reflection, feel that my decision was right. I know I am ready to move on, to take up a new life and stay active.

The hardest part is saying goodbye to the AFB Board of Trustees and the beautiful staff we have here at AFB. I thank the Board of Trustees for their support and guidance, and the staff for their wonderful cooperation during my 19 years at AFB. And then, I must thank you, the readers of AFB NEWS, who have never failed to let me know when my opinions were on target or off.

I look forward to my retirement. And I know from hearing from my friends in Massachusetts, that I will stay active – whether it is taking on new assignments with some of the agencies for the blind, or having season tickets for the football and basketball games at my alma mater, Holy Cross. It will be a new lifestyle, but a challenge, and as some of you may know, I enjoy a new challenge.

I am going to miss each and every one of you. And as someone once said, 'it is not goodbye, but just so long.' I will see all of you in my heart. Thanks!

THE LAKE

In 1972, Bill and Kay Gallagher purchased a beautiful piece of property on the shores of Webster Lake in Webster, Massachusetts. The land was on a peninsula that extended a fair distance into the Lake itself and their property was located at the end of the peninsula. Bill bought the property for a song. Over the years, there were improvements made and the quarters became much more liveable.

Buying the property was by far the best investment that Bill ever made in his life as it was in this place that Kay and Bill spent the happiest years of their lives. It was their home away from home, the place where the two spent holidays and weekends and vacations at the site. There were two cottages on the premises and a never ending stream of friends who came and went, enjoying the cook outs, the fishing and the swimming. It was always open house at Gallagher's place on the peninsula, with children more than welcome at all times.

Webster Lake, in the Town of Webster, is not the true name of the Lake. The true name is an Indian name, given to the Lake by the Nipmuck Indians, who lived there long ago. It is spelled as follows:

CHARGOGGAGGOGGMANCHAUGGAGGOGGCHAUBUNA GUNGAMAUGG.

The name is translated as follows into English:

You fish on your side

I fish on my side

Nobody fishes in the middle.

An article in the <u>New York Times</u>, November 20, 2004, by Pam Belluck, entitled, "What's the Name of That Lake? It's Hard to

Rocks: The Blind Guy at the Lake

Say" begins with the name of the Lake: Lake Chargoggagoggmanchauggagogghaubunagungamaugg. She adds: "It is spelled just as it sounds."

There are different spellings of the Lake in the area itself. The local chamber of commerce has a different spelling from that found in post-cards "at Water Front Mary's the Lake's best known restaurant."

Pam writes: "Gone are the years Ethel Merman and Ray Bolger made it a name you could dance to in a tune called "The Lake Song."

Oh we took a walk one evening and we sat down on a log by Lake Chargoggagoggmanchauggagogghaubunagungamaugg. Chargoggagoggmanchauggagogghaubunagungamaugg,

There, we told love's old sweet story and we listened to a frog in Lake Chargoggagoggmanchauggagogghaubunagungamaugg Chargoggagoggmanchauggagogghaubunagungamaugg.

Bill's very close friend, Bob Johnson, relates a great story that goes with the Lake's Indian name. It seems that one night, at a local bar, there was a discussion among the customers about the name. One of the customers was a stranger to this area. He claimed that he could pronounce the name with ease. The local said to him, "Oh yeah?" "I can not only pronounce the name, but I can spell it as well."

"You can, can you?" "I am holding a copy of the spelling right here in my hand. If you can pronounce the name which I know well, and then spell it, I'll buy the house a drink."

"You're on," said the local.

He pronounced the name with ease. Now, came the tough part. There are forty-five letters in the name, twenty-two of which are consonants and twenty-three of which are vowels. The local began to spell the name – slowly, but surely. Hesitating here and there, he spelled the name perfectly. The stranger slammed his money on the bar, paid for the house's drink and stormed out.

Bob Johnson said, "What the stranger did not know was that the name was spelled out in large letters on a poster that hung on the wall right over his head and behind him." The local, as he spelled out the name, slowly but surely took many a glance at the poster to make sure that he was spelling the name correctly.

One of Bill's favorite past-times at the cottages was playing cribbage. He was a great cribbage player. He needed Braille cards to play the game. He got mad when some players substituted regular cards for the Braille cards. Bob Johnson said that Bill was an excellent player because he was able to memorize all the numbers.

Bob Johnson's wife, Flo remembers how much Bill enjoyed to go fishing in Webster Lake. She said: "I would bait Bill's hook with a worm. He could make a cast and have a fish on the end of his hook before I was able to bait my own hook. Most often, he would bring in a blue gill or a trout; sometimes, a perch or a pickerel. After he made his cast, he held his fingers on the line. When he felt the pull of the fish, he would reel it in. He said that he would use this experience in his rehabilitation course. Fishing was one of Bill's great joys."

As for the food and drink at the Lake, there was plenty of it. Most of the food was buffet style. Kay could care less about cooking. There was plenty of beer to drink to wash the food down. Kay loved her beer. By Sunday, if they ran out of food, Bill and a few others would go into town to purchase food to carry them over for the day. Bill had a particular fondness for Chinese food.

Bill loved his music and spent hours listening to his vast collection. Carl Augusto recalled one weekend, Bill and Kay invited him and his wife Sue to join them at their summer home in Lake Webster. When they arrived, a Frank Sinatra phonograph was playing. "Frank Sinatra was with us the entire weekend. Sue and Carl vowed they'd never listen to Frank Sinatra again. Incidentally, maybe because of Bill's influence, they become a big Frank Sinatra fan."

As an indication of Bill's and Kay's generosity, they had eighteen keys to the house made for their closest friends. One time, they all got caught in a snow storm and the entire eighteen had to sleep over, which did not bother Bill one bit.

Among the guests at the Lake, there was a great diversity of ethnic groups: Jewish, Armenian, Dutch, Polish, Irish, English, and more. At one of these gatherings, one of the guests told a Polish joke, which was not flattering to the Polish people. Bill quietly, but firmly, said to this person, "You don't have to bother doing that again." Everyone got the message. Bill did not like ethnic jokes.

****

When Bill and Kay purchased their place on Webster Lake, their good friends John and Ann Kelly visited them quite often. John recalls: "From the top of the peninsula at night-fall, you would see the most beautiful sunsets imaginable across the Lake, as the sun went down over the mountains. By this time in our lives, we had two children, Bill and John. They were little tots, 2 ½ and 4 years of age. Both of the boys idolized Bill and Kay, calling them ever and always Uncle Bill and Aunt Kay.

So often over the years, we heard the clarion call from Bill, "Come on up. Bring the boys." Sometimes we might come up for just a weekend. Often enough, we would stay for a week or more. Whenever Bill and Kay needed to go shopping, we drove them to their destinations. On these excursions, Kay would buy anything that the boys wanted. At Sears, she would buy them toys of all descriptions. She always treated them to ice cream.

One day when things were quiet at the Lake and our boys were still quite young, one of them said to Kay: "Do you need anything from Sears today?" Bill nearly died laughing when he heard that one.

One of Bill's neighbors purchased a brand new motorboat. This neighbor knew little or nothing about boats and less about motors. One bright day, he took everyone for a ride, Bill included. Bill felt uneasy in the boat and the next time he was offered a ride, he declined to go. Sure enough on that occasion, the motor went dead in the middle of the Lake. The owner had a fancy up-to-date tool box on board, which he put to work, but to no avail. The man could hardly tell the difference between a wrench and a screw driver. There was only one solution to the problem. The neighbor began using paddles to row the boat into shore. Before he began to row, he placed his fancy tool box on the bow of the boat in a precarious position. My boys were standing with Bill on the shore describing to him all that was happening. When the boat neared the shore, Bill yelled out to the paddler: "How is that tool box working my friend?" No sooner were the words out of Bill's mouth when the fancy tool box tipped over into the water with a great splash, followed by a stream of loud curses from the owner. Bill laughed so hard he was bent over.

I can tell you one thing about Bill. By nature, he loved to laugh.

****

John and Ann Kelly's two sons, William and John, also have fond memories of the two people they came to call Uncle Bill and Aunt Kay from the outset of their relationship, which began in 1973 and lasted until both Bill and Kay passed away.

William remembers:

"As a boy, I was a very insecure kid. Besides my Mom and Dad, Bill and Kay were the only other adults who made me feel both loved and respected. They treated you like you really mattered to them, no matter what your age was. This had a profound impact on me, as I was growing up from boyhood to manhood.

At night time, a ritual was established when it came time for us to go to bed, after an evening of listening to Bill's music with Bill and Kay, Mom and Dad and my brother, John. Bill would say:

Rocks: The Blind Guy at the Lake

"Time to turn in – Will you have some ice cream with me?" Of course, we never refused his generous offer. He then gave us ice cream cones and a glass of milk. Pecan was Bill's favorite.

His last words might be: "Does anyone mind if when I jump into bed, I turn the radio on to listen to the Red Sox game?" He would fall off to sleep, listening to his beloved Red Sox doing their best in victory or defeat. He was able to picture what was going on in the game based on his memory of playing sand-lot baseball before he was blinded.

Very often at the Lake, Bill would spend time listening to books recorded on tape. Nothing would please him more than to have you sitting beside him listening to the tapes as well.

It never ceased to amaze me how Uncle Bill was able to meet the challenge of blindness and go on to affect the lives of countless thousands for the better, who had suffered a similar fate to his own. Uncle Bill was the kindest, most gentle person I ever knew. Even as a young boy, I was completely in awe of him. He was the toughest man I ever met. He was a giant.

Webster Lake was a paradise for my brother and I. We swam in crystal clear water. Great fishing was available to us. We went on boat rides and we met so many interesting people from all walks of life. The Gallaghers gave us a great gift. They made us feel that their home was our home.

Aunt Kay was one of the most generous people I ever knew. When we went to the market with her, she had a standing offer – you can have anything you want. She was a great listener. She was so interested in the stories you had to tell. Aunt Kay never tried to placate you. All she wanted was that you should be yourself. She was very smart – a woman of high intelligence. As a story teller, she was nonpareil. I loved her very much and still do.

Much of what William's brother John remembers about Bill and Kay is reflected in the words of his brother William. He adds, "When I was not much more than a toddler, I knew that Bill and

Kay were very special. One day, I was digging while in a kneeling position on the ground, as boys are known to do. Kay came along. I said to her: "Would you like to dig with me?" Without a moment's hesitation, she knelt down beside me and there were the two of us, digging away.

I have thought about which of my senses I would choose to lose, if such a decision was forced on me. My choice might well be my sight, simply because of the example that Bill Gallagher was to me. He had an incredibly perceptive and rewarding life. He traveled the nation and the world without a cane. He spoke before committees of the United States Congress. He was the recipient of a Presidential Citation. He mingled with celebrities. He mingled with the common man. He was friend and inspiration to them all. He inherited Helen Keller's desk at the American Foundation for the Blind. He up-lifted all who came to know him. He helped the blind to "see." He was a man for all seasons.

Bill and Kay had that rare ability to make you feel welcome and at home. When the Kelly family was at the Lake, each one of us felt that we were part of the Gallager Family. That is the effect that they had on you.

Were William and John the children that Bill and Kay never had?

****

A great party to celebrate Bill's 70th Birthday was held at the Lake. The Kelly family composed the lyrics of a song for the occasion, sung to the tune of <u>Let Me Call You Sweetheart</u>.

We met you out in Pittsburgh
When we didn't have a dime
But you and Kay together
Made sure that we had a good time
Then along came a place called Lake Webster
And your friends so tried and true
And we're glad that Midge invited us

Rocks: The Blind Guy at the Lake

To be here with you
To be here with you

So happy birthday to Bill Gallagher
From your friends both far and near
We're thrilled to be here with you
Celebrating your 70th year
Thank you for your friendship
And your helpful giving ways
We wish you health and happiness
For the remainder of your days.

****

Some men have a phenomenal ability to be able to fix anything. Joe Kmiotek was such a handyman. If anything needed fixing at Bill's cottage and later at the dream house, Joe was "Johnny on the Spot." He fixed the lawnmower when it went on the blink. A broken window was no problem for him to repair. If an electric wire needed replacing, Joe became Bill's electrician. Joe took care of mowing the lawn and painting, wherever and whenever it was needed. Joe and his wife Shirley were two of the best friends and neighbors that Bill and Kay ever had at the Lake.

Joe remembers:

Our friendship with Bill and Kay began when we met them through mutual friends. They told us about Bill, the blind man, who had a place in Webster, Massachusetts on Webster Lake. We were invited to a party to meet Bill and Kay. We soon found out that they were people that we got to like. After the party, Bill said for us to come any time, even without an invitation, when they were at the Lake. That was an open invitation, which lasted for thirty (30) years.

After a few months, Kay gave me a key to the cottage, so we could enjoy the Lake, fishing, swimming and boating, even when they were not there.

Rocks: The Blind Guy at the Lake

On weekends when Bill and Kay would fly into Worcester from New York City, we would pick them up and bring them to the Lake. Some weekends, we would stay with them. When the weekend was over, we would drive them back to the airport. This went on for years.

In summers, if Bill had a conference to attend, he and Kay would invite us to go with them for a week, if our vacation time permitted it. We would agree to go, but only on the condition that we would pay our own way.

Shirley recalled the Las Vega trip in particular. They saw so many places of interest, including Salt Lake City, where they spent four days. From there they flew onto Denver. Bill had a conference in Toronto at the time, and while he was gone, we stayed in his suite at the hotel. While we were there, we took care of furnishing the snacks and serving the drinks for colleagues and friends of Bill, who dropped by.

Many hours were spent listening to Bill's music. He was particularly fond of the music of the Big Bands so popular in that era. Bill had hundreds of cassettes. Evenings were never dull. Cribbage was the game of choice. It was Bill who was always first to count his cards. Shirley, my wife, did not play the game at first, never having played it before. By watching Bill play, she learned how to play the game. Soon, she became as sharp as Bill at the game.

At the Lake before he went to bed, he would always ask, "Who is on for some ice cream, peanuts, and a few saltines."

None of us will ever forget two of the finest people that God ever put on the face of the earth.

****

There was a tavern on the opposite shore from Bill's place known as Waterfront Mary's. At the time, the bar had a sand floor and had been described as "the kind of place where you'd buy only cans of beer and wipe them off before you'd drink" them. On occasion, Bill and others would travel over to Waterfront Mary's by pontoon boat for a few bottles of beer. Mary was a buxom, well-preserved lady, who, wore grass skirts or leotard print outfits and distributed silly hats and tambourines to patrons who sat on chairs made from saddles and toilet seats and ate on tables made from bath tubs. Upon seeing Bill, Mary would always rush over to him and give him the biggest hug that any man on earth ever received. That great hug and squeeze left Bill blushing a very bright red. But it did not deter him from visiting Waterfront Mary's over the years.

****

Not too long before Bill retired from the American Foundation for the Blind, he and Kay talked about building a fine home on their Lake property. The idea they had was to gut the structures already on the property and build their dream house on Webster Lake, where they would live out their retirement years. It was one of Kay's fondest wishes to have such a home.

Brian Sutor, was a talented and widely recognized architect. He and his wife Ann were neighbors of Bill and Kay at the Lake, and were among their closest friends. Sutor volunteered to design the house. Brian not only drew the plans for the house, he personally supervised the building of the structure on a daily basis. Bill and Kay gave him a free rein to come up with something nice, because they loved his house, even the outside color scheme.

With the foundation in place, tragedy struck. Kay passed away on November 17, 1990, long before the house was finished. God alone, can measure the sorrow that was in Bill's heart at this great loss, just before his and Kay's dream came true.

****

Following Kay's death, the AFB received so many contributions in Kay's name that it established the Kay Gallagher Award. Carl Augusto explains that Bill wanted that money to go to young blind people because he said Kay was always on the lookout for up-and-comers that he could support and mentor.

AFB ESTABLISHES KAY GALLAGHER MENTOR FUND

NEW YORK – AFB has established a special fund in memory of Catherine T. "Kay" Gallagher, wife of AFB President and Executive Director William F. Gallagher, who died November 17, 1990. The Kay Gallagher Fund will be used to recognize congenitally blind individuals who have demonstrated exemplary participation in the workplace and the community and have served as role models for other blind and visually impaired persons.

Said Gallagher: "Whenever Kay met young blind and visually impaired persons, she always remarked that she hoped they had good role models who would motivate and inspire them to be all that they could be in life. She believed wholeheartedly in the importance of mentors in the lives of all people. The Kay Gallagher Mentor Award will recognize blind persons who have served as mentors for so many others – blind and sighted."

Kay Gallagher was, herself, a mentor in many ways. As an Assistant Professor of Nursing at the Borough of Manhattan Community College, she specialized in programs that recruit and train minority students in the field of nursing, and was a past recipient of the School of Nursing Professor of the Year Award.

Years earlier, Kay served as a lieutenant in the U.S. Army Nurse Corps during the Korean Conflict, working out of the original Mobile Army Surgical Hospital (MASH) unit during 1951-1952. She retired from the Army Reserve with the rank of Captain.

Following Bill's death, AFB renamed the fund the Bill and Kay Gallagher Award and has given the award, a plaque and a $1,000.00 gift, to nearly ten blind people.

****

John Kelly believes that Bill lost his will to live after Kay died. He remembers, "Bill had a great love for steak, which Kay cut up for him in small pieces. He was a big eater, but after Kay died, you would have to force him even to eat a peanut butter and jelly sandwich. At one sitting, Bill would often eat a whole pizza pie. With Kay gone from the scene, he would barely eat one slice."

Flo Johnson remembered that the day a friend had asked Bill how he and Kay got together. He answered: "It was not love at first sight. It was love at first touch." Bob added, "These two love birds, when they were at the Lake, were always the first up on Sunday morning, so that they could get to Sunday Mass at the local church. They never missed."

****

When Kay passed, Bill was undecided whether to finish building his and Kay's dream house. After a short while, he said that he wanted to finish building the house. He decided that everything in the cottage had to go. A dumpster came and took it all away, except for the cribbage table, which Joe took home and refinished.

Bill was deeply involved in the selection as to size, design, scheme and color. He felt each item with his hands and either approved or disapproved the item in question. When the house was ready for occupancy, Brian took Bill on a tour of the house. By and by, some friends came to see the house. Much to Brian's amazement, Bill took his visitors on exactly the same tour that Brian directed a short time before, and he did this without a hitch and without Brian helping in any way. This was not an ordinary house. It was more like a mansion with many, many rooms. The room in the house which came to be known as "Gallagher's Pub" was 40' by 15' with a bar at one end. The color motif was Kelly green to give it an Irish flavor to the scheme, as Bill was very proud to be Irish.

Before the construction of the house had begun, Brian mentioned that a friend of his had a hot tub installed in his house, which included jets and a whirlpool. He thought that Rocks might be interested in having such a tub in his new house. Bill said "Let's go and see it." After they saw it, Bill said "I want one of those."

Rocks: The Blind Guy at the Lake

The new house had great picture windows on the ground floor, looking out on to the Lake. He filled the walls with plaques, awards and mementos from his travels. Bill would look out of the upper level slider and say "What a view we have, the best on Webster Lake!!"

****

One day at the Lake, Bill was sitting on his porch, relaxing in the quiet of the scene, overlooking the Lake. Suddenly, he heard loud screaming. Two voices were pleading "Save us! Save us!"

Bill waded out into the water up to his arm pits in the direction of the screaming.

What had happened Bill found out later was that these two people were in a canoe which had tipped over. Neither one of them could swim. They were hanging onto the canoe for their dear lives. Bill sized up the situation. He took hold of one end of the canoe and pulled it into dry land, thus saving two lives.

The reader might recall that before Bill was blinded, he saved a young swimmer from drowning.

****

After Kay passed away, Midge, Kay's sister, continued to live with Rocks to care for him. Midge had promised Kay on her death bed that she would continue to live with Bill and take care of him in his declining years. Midge passed away on April 15, 1997.

****

Tom Costello remembers an incident that occurred about a month before the Class of '48's 50th Reunion. It bound him to Rocks forever.

Tom had not attended a reunion from the 25th to the 45th, having had a falling out with the administration at the College. After a classmate's urging, he had attended the 45th. That turned out to be a mistake. He received a cold shoulder from many of his classmates in attendance, and he decided then and there, that he would never again darken Holy Cross's doorstep.

The 50th Reunion came along and Tom Costello continued to be adamant that he would not attend, despite phone calls from different classmates, like his good friend Larry Cantwell.

Then, one day, he received a telephone call from Rocks. "Tom, this is Rocks Gallagher. I am calling to ask you to attend our 50th Reunion. I would like very much for you to sit at my table at our reunion dinner."

Tom was absolutely stunned. His mind was already made up. God could not make him go to this reunion.

Then suddenly it hit him. This is the one man in the entire world to whom he could not say "No." And just as suddenly, he came to realize how much he loved this "Man For All Seasons." He recalls that he went to that reunion, sat with "Rocks" and enjoyed those few days immensely. He never saw Rocks alive again.

THE FINAL YEARS – DEATH COMES TO ROCKS

Bill Gallagher, in the final stages of his life, suffered from Parkinson's Disease.

Tom Sullivan, although appearing hale and hearty, has been diagnosed with Parkinson's Disease. He acknowledges: "I have been able to accept it and deal with it because of the example Billy showed me in dealing with the same disease."

****

When interviewed by well known columnist Frances Fiset as a freshman at Holy Cross, Bill Gallagher gave the following advice to Sighted People:

> *When talking or writing to a person who is blind, don't be afraid to mention the words sight, blind, eyes or words of color. Deliberately bring them into use as soon as possible. If they are constantly avoided, the language is apt to become stilted and awkward and everyone is uncomfortable.*

> *I enjoy movies through companionship, hearing and the picture I see in my mind's eye, I like to be asked if I enjoy seeing a picture. To be asked if I enjoy "hearing" it, makes me feel isolated.*

Father Carroll stated that Bill Gallagher, the war blind and other blind persons, have been given a handicap, but he has a favorite definition for that word. A handicap is a weight placed by God on the shoulders of a superior person to make the race more even.

Tom Costello believes that Rocks Gallagher was such a superior person. He states, "In my own mind, God chooses certain individuals to suffer through a handicap so that they will develop the wherewithal to help those who are similarly handicapped. Rocks Gallagher spent his life doing for others what was done for him in his journey to be fully rehabilitated. And, therein, lies his true greatness and inspiring contribution to the blinded community. He gave back what he was given one hundred fold." Tom Costello recalls that Bill had a quality of endurance and resiliency, which he often spoke to Frank Marshall about, as Rocks stubbornly hung onto life even as it was slowly ebbing out of him. When Frank would speak about how weak Rocks had become, only to seem to bounce back again and again, Tom commented that, in addition to all his other great qualities, Rocks was one tough old guy. Tom finishes, "And, so he was. We will all miss him. He taught all of us so much about how to live. Neither the 1948 Classmates, nor Holy Cross, will ever see his like again."

****

After Midge passed, Bill had three care-takers around the clock who looked after him. At this stage, he was a very lonesome man.

Anne and John Kelly visited with Bill several times a month, sometimes bringing their sons. They sang the old songs Rocks enjoyed so much:

The Apple Sauce:

Apple Sauce oh apple sauce
That's all they eat at Holy Cross
The eat it morning, noon and night
They even eat it when they're tight
Oh apple sauce, oh apple sauce
That's all they eat at Holy Cross
(Sung to the melody of Oh Christmas Tree – Oh
Tannenbaum)

Mamie Reilly: (Rock's true favorite)

Oh Mamie Reilly how do you do today
Oh Mamie Reilly going far away
Come and kiss your Daddy
Before you depart
Oh Mamie, Mamie, Mamie Reilly
Slide Kelly slide – Casey's at the bat
Oh Mamie Reilly where'd you get that hat
Down in old Kentucky, old black Joe
Oh Mamie, Mamie, Mamie Reilly
Ho! (in a very loud voice)

On one occasion when Bill was not quite up to par John
Kelly who knew many, many songs by heart and who had a fairly
good voice, offered to sing a few songs for Rocks to pick him up,
"very few" said Bill in typical fashion – raising his eyebrows a
notch to reveal in the surprising blue eyes the sparkle that blindness
and illness never eclipsed.

When the house had been completed, Joe had brought back
the refurbished cribbage table. Midge, Bill's sister-in-law, said it
was a masterpiece. However, it was seldom used when Bill became
very sick. One day, he asked Joe to be its caretaker. Now, when
Joe walks by it, he thinks of Bill, Kay and Midge, and all the happy

hours he and Shirley had with them.

Toward the end, Bill was admitted to a nursing home which he very much disliked. So he returned home under the care of his nurses. With all the sorrow in his life at this stage, he did his very best to remain upbeat. Toward the end, his condition deteriorated to such an extent that it became necessary to hire three nurses, who stayed with him and cared for him around the clock, seven days a week.

Elizabeth ("Betty") Vinton was one of the nurses who captured in her beautiful recollection the true essence of Rocks. She wrote: The Blind Guy at the Lake. . . Bill Gallagher was a little intimidating when I first interviewed with him. Bill was in need of extreme physical care, yet at the same time, his mind was alert, he was intelligent, and he had the most intense blue eyes. Thankfully, we enjoyed three years of a special relationship, a dual bond of care-giver and friendship.

Bill was very fond of his former wife, Kay. 'It was love at first touch,' he would often remark. Each time Bill would tell of how they met and their life together, a soft smile would cross his face. He was so proud of her achievements and glowed when he spoke of her. When Bill would wake from a nap, or when he woke in the middle of the night and he needed something, he would call out to "Kay," then, quickly realizing what he had done, he would apologize. It must have been too painful for Bill to speak of her becoming ill and losing her. He never spoke of their last days together.

Bill had friends, lots of them and he loved and appreciated each one - A one-man United Nations of love and acceptance. He considered each one worthy of the others friendship. He loved the telephone calls, the get-togethers, and many times, planned special events, to have a reason to see them. Age and the debilitating progressiveness of Parkinson's had robbed him of this joy. Bill shared his beautiful home, as well as his heart, with his friends and was thrilled to have them stay with him.

Bill was introduced to country western music and began to look forward to Saturday evenings so we could "watch" the Statler Brothers and The Grand Ole' Opry.

Bill looked forward to Sundays and the sports-in season. He taught me about golf so that I actually began to appreciate it. When he was still sighted, he would ride his bike to the golf course and be a caddy for a day, and hoped to one day master the game himself. He was challenged by a friend to a round of golf. Bill said the only way to level the playing field, was to play at midnight. The challenge was retracted.

We watched all of the basketball games. The Boston Celtics, and, of course, the Holy Cross games. He enjoyed telling how he became the team 'mascot." He had an interest in football. Football was so intensely listened to by Bill, he would often exclaim, "That must have hurt," even before the announcer had told of the blitz or pile up.

As Bill's care-giver, the most obvious challenge was to begin healing his excoriated, raw, neglected wounds. When I asked him if he was up to the challenge, he would answer "We'll do our best," and wryly smile. I told him he was allowed to scream and even swear, but he was not allowed to whine. He never did.

Four P.M. (on the minute) was the specified time for Seagram's 7 with two or three ice cubes in a 4 oz. glass. No more than three ice cubes or 'you are fired.' He told me more than a few times, that if I were to do so, 'I would be missed.'

Bill liked to have the newspapers read to him, especially articles about 'The Lake' or sports in season, primarily anything and everything that had to do with Holy Cross. He would have articles sent to Frank that were of special interest.

His last night – I was thankful to be the one with him – he was so frail as I changed his position to make him more comfortable. He asked me to make him some oatmeal. I told him it was 1:30 in the morning, but if he wanted some, I would be glad to make some. As I walked to the kitchen, I could hear him breathing through the monitor. I took a chair and returned to him. Sitting close and holding his hand, he looked at me for a moment with those most intense blue eyes, and then went to sleep.

I am thankful and honored to have had the opportunity of being his care-giver, and to have been introduced to his life and friends.

****

I have fought the good fight:

I have finished my course:

I have kept the faith

2 Tim 4:7

The Man Born Blind: And as he was passing by, he saw a man blind from birth. And his disciples asked him "Rabbi, who has sinned, this man or his parents, that he should be born blind?" Jesus answered: "Neither has this man sinned, nor his parents, but the works of God were to be made manifest in him." St. John 9:1-3.

Rocks: The Blind Guy at the Lake

Sunset

The Great man had passed away.

No longer would he, lonely be

Without his beloved Kay

Together now they would see the glorious sunset

Over the western mountains of Webster Lake

Hand in Hand, Hearts entwined

Forever more – forever more."

-Thomas P. Costello

Domini dilexi decorum
Tuae et locum habit -
Ationis gloriae tuea
I have loved, O Lord,
The beauty of thy house
And the place wherein
Thy glory dwelleth

(Ps 25:8, the Lavabo Psalm)

Rocks: The Blind Guy at the Lake

Requiem aeternam dona ei,
Domine, et Lux Perpetua
Luceat ei, Requiescat in
Pace Amen
Eternal rest grant unto him,
O Lord and may perpetual light
Shine upon him
May he rest in peace Amen.

Rocks: The Blind Guy at the Lake

THE FUNERAL

Rocks passed away on April 24, 2000. His funeral Mass was held at Sacred Heart of Jesus Church, Worcester, Massachusetts. Father John E. Brooks, S.J., President Emeritus of Holy Cross College and a student at the college during the years Rocks was there as well, delivered a very moving homily at the Mass.

My brothers and sisters in the Lord: It is with sincere thanks and abundant praise that I proclaim the 'Good News' to you this morning. Thanks to all of you for having taken the time to join us for this celebration marking Rocks Gallagher's passage from this life through death to a fully graced and blessed life forever in the presence of our loving God. And praise to this same God – our generous, forgiving and loving Father – for the wonderful gift He has given us over the years in the person of Rocks. Your presence here this morning is indeed a source of comfort and consolation to Rocks' sister, Mary Langan, his nephews and nieces, as well as to Father Frank Miller and myself who, in our long association with the College of the Holy Cross, Rocks' Alma Mater, have enjoyed a warm friendship with Rocks. We are deeply grateful to you!

In a highly dramatic passage introducing the 6th Chapter of the Book of Micah, there is vividly portrayed for us a courtroom scene in which there are three main figures: (1) the prophet Micah; (2) Yahweh (God), the Plaintiff; and (3) the People of Judah, the Defendants.

The scene opens with the figure of Yahweh acting as a pleader in Court. He calls upon the 'mountains,' the 'hills' and the very 'foundations of the earth' to be witnesses to the case He has against His people. And he goes on to indict the Kingdom of Judah, not by detailing its offenses and crimes, but rather by reciting a few of the Exodus events, i.e., by recalling His own acts of justice and mercy, and grace and love, toward His people – acts which should have evoked, but did not, a similar response from God's covenanted people.

The text reads:

O my people, what have I done to you? In what way have I wearied you? Answer me! For I brought you up from the Land of Egypt and I redeemed you from the house of bondage; And I sent before you Moses, Aaron and Miriam. O my people, remember what Balak, King of Moab counseled, and what Balaam, son of Beor answered. Remember your journey from Shittim to Gilgal, that you may know the saving acts of the Lord. (Micah 6:3-5).

Then the people o Judah, citing specific forms of sacrifice, inquire as to how they might return to a state of friendship with God. Should they come before Him and win His favor with burnt offerings? With the sacrificial slaying of lambs? With rivers of oil? Or possibly even with the sacrifice of their first-born children? In each instance, the response is a firm and resounding 'NO" – God is not interested in empty, meaningless sacrifice – mere external forms with no corresponding interior disposition.

Then the prophet Micah, addressing the people, cries out, "It has already been told you what is good," and he goes on to tell the people

*unequivocally that to "return" to God, a man must
do right, love steadfastly, and walk humbly with his
God, i.e., he must be a just and fair man – just and
fair in his dealings with other men and women, with
his family, his fellow workers and his friends; he
must reciprocate God's love – he must love as God
loves, and he must have a "right" relationship with
God, i.e., he must strive to live in a state of
friendship with God.*

****

Frank Marshall '48 was one of Rocks' closest friends, especially in Bill's waning years. There was no one in the Class of '48 who did more for Rocks to comfort and assist him as he prepared to meet his Maker. It was fitting that Frank was chosen to give the Eulogy for Rocks. Frank's beautiful testament to his best friend:

Father Brooks, Father Miller, Father Bartlett, Bill's sister Mary, relatives and friends. We join in tribute to the glory contained in Bill Gallagher and shared by him with all he knew. He truly was a treasure for all fortunate enough to pass his way. We reflect on the man, the heart, the courage, the accomplishment, the wit, the faithfulness, as well as his acceptance and resignation.

Bill Gallagher enjoyed several lives. One began the morning he awoke blind. That is the life most of us know. Though sightless, Bill saw a lot more than most of us. He knew, as few of us do, what life is all about – and he exemplified life. He was the one who encouraged his parents that they could handle his loss, they could live through it.

Bill adjusted well and quickly – becoming captain of The Perkins School for the Blind wrestling team. Fortunately for us, his dear friend, Father Carroll deflected him from Boston College toward the College of the Holy Cross, where the mutual love affair bloomed fast and fully. It blossomed with his roommate, Bill Furlong, who besides being Bill's roommate, was perhaps best remembered for an election and for renaming Bill. In election debate, Furlong's opponent suggested no one would want to vote for a man who put his dirty clothes in a blind man's laundry bag for his mother to wash! Though classically true, Furlong's girlfriend lived near the Gallaghers and he stayed there more than Bill. The election was over, Furlong lost to the laundry bag. That gave him more time to watch Bill like a hawk, leading him to catching Bill stealing a roll from the next table. "Gallagher," he screamed, "you're as bad as the thief in the book I am reading. His name is "Rocks" – we ought to call you "Rocks" – and we have forevermore. At Holy Cross, there is only Rocks Gallagher. A classmate asked me last week what his real first name is.

One may feel we are not mournful enough today but Bill was a celebration of life and his humor perhaps bridged the gap and contributed mightily to one of the finest lives we have had the good grace of God to know. The more you know Bill, the more you realize and appreciate how extraordinary he was. In addition to enjoying the Beatific Vision, he now sees his beloved Kay for the first time!! He always saw but not as we see. He was such that even Kay would forget. Soon after moving into their new apartment, Kay went into the hall to test the security. Ringing the bell, she asked Rocks if he could see her through the peep hole in the door – "No," he replied, "I've never seen you."

He sees her now – so please be happy for him. Humor highlights how extraordinarily gifted Bill Gallagher is, beyond any human measure. We all, I trust, have the privilege of knowing a few exceptional people in our lives and Bill is one of such a handful.

All of us here today have the privilege of knowing Bill Gallagher, some more fortunate than others. The better one knows Bill, the more they love him, respect him, admire him, are inspired by him. Bill made a difference. I am confident he continues to make a difference for the rest of our lives.

Rocks: The Blind Guy at the Lake

We say this because if we are close to Bill, we had the grace to learn from him what life is all about. We had the opportunity to learn the meaning of trust, compassion, accomplishment, modesty, smiling at adversity without ever once, to my knowledge, complaining. Not when he woke up blind in the prime of his youth, not when his friend, aid, eyes and the love of his life, Kay, was taken from him. Not later when he arrived alone at the beautiful Webster Lake home he and Kay had so much fun planning and building together. Not when he could hardly lift his head and smile during those last days as he lay in the hospital, fading away before our eyes. Perhaps his last burst of response and enthusiasm was when his dear friend, John Kelly, sang "Ole Mamie Reilly" to him. Bill is our patron saint of truly accepting God's will with courage.

Speaking of Holy Cross and "Ole Mamie Reilly," we cannot speak of Bill without Holy Cross. His fellow Crusaders gave Bill their elbows but they did not carry him, nor would have let them. They let him go home alone after an evening's relaxation, to be left off at the wrong location, onto the icy walkway and become lost for the only time in his four years at Holy Cross.

They cheated him at Salt Shakers – telling him he had slid his shaker off the far end of the table when he knew it had stopped ½ inch from the edge, thereby beating his opponent who really did go over.

Which all helped Rocks adjust to the more competitive world beyond Perkins and Holy Cross. But we did not cheat him out of traveling with the basketball team and helping inspire them to winning the NCAA championship. And Bill always saw the game and watched it on TV – he never said he "listened." He went on to become the only blind member of the Holy Cross Athletic Hall of Fame.

Who present will forget his standing ovation as the featured speaker at the 25th reunion of his Class of '48? Bill went on to even greater fame in the evermore competitive world beyond Perkins and Holy Cross. He devoted his life to inspiring the disabled,

Page 156

particularly blind and sight-impaired people, to a more productive, fulfilled life. From caseworker to the top position in the field of blindness in the United States, as President and Executive Director of the American Foundation for the Blind, he pioneered advances in aiding the handicapped through the United States and much of the world. With lesser commitment to the American Federation, he would have been President of the World Blind Union. The Foundation requested that he decline the invitation to become President of the World Blind Union feeling that they could not afford the time, energy and travel that would be required of Rocks in his capacity as President of the World Blind Union. Rocks acceded to the Foundation's request.

In his nomination for an honorary degree at Holy Cross, the list of organizations he served is incredibly extensive and impressive. The awards he earned fill a full typewritten page.

Perhaps the greatest challenge in his life of human service was balancing his primary responsibility as head of the AFB with demands to step out form behind his – and formerly Helen Keller's desk, to share his inspirational assistance, leadership, teaching or message to other service organizations of all varieties. Frequently accomplishing the impossible, he, over many years, traveled more than one hundred thousand (100,000) miles throughout the United States and abroad to Russia, Australia, New Zealand, Canada, Spain, France, Germany, England and Ireland. He was a giant. He's our modest, dearest friend. He's a saint – the man, the heart, the spirit and the daily blessing to all who knew him - Holy Cross College of the Extraordinary, Father Brooks, Father Miller, others you know but NONE more so than Rocks. And a special vote of thanks to the dedicated ladies who cared for Rocks over the last several years with such skill and love – Bette, Sharon and Pam.

Father Frank Miller's last message to Rocks was "prayers and love forever." From us also, Father.

Rocks: The Blind Guy at the Lake

Tom Costello closed with the poetic tribute he had written for Rocks.

ROCKS

We gather here

this Spring-time morn

Not as men sad or forlorn

for loss of our laughing smiling boy

But in celebration of a life

That gave each one of us

a sense of joy.

Rocks was our shining star

And so it is on this day

Our Class of '48 has come

From near and far

To honor him and to

Remember him

For his gift of courage

of inspiration and of love.

The Psalmist said:

"They have eyes to see
but see not"

Rocks had eyes

that could not see

But he saw all in life

That was beautiful and true.

In Psalm 146 we read:

"He tells the number of stars,

He calls each by name"

Now God has a new name to call

Known by one and all

Of the Class of '48

ROCKS GALLAGHER

One of our very own

At long last our smiling boy

Is at home.

A lovely and creative touch was provided by Leon Bartholomew as the casket was being wheeled down the center aisle of Sacred Heart Church. He handed his Holy Cross cap with a prominent "HC" on it to Bill Cahill, who gently placed it on the casket as it went by. At the services at the nearby St. John Mausoleum, the cap was still on the bier and was interred with our beloved classmate.

At the close of the interment services, we all sang the alma mater. It was an emotional moment for all who were there and a fitting conclusion to what all of us felt was a marvelous sendoff for the old Rocker. Following the internment, the classmates joined the Gallagher family members for a convivial luncheon at a Webster Square restaurant. After lunch and before leaving, Bob Mulcahy led the classmates in a rendering of "Ole Mamie Reilly!" We all felt that Rocks would be very pleased with the entire proceedings of the day. There was so much that could be said about our recollections, but again, it is almost impossible to add to the tributes of John Brooks, Frank Marshall and Tom Costello. At the same time, there are countless cherished remembrances of this great man.

EPILOGUE

Who of us who were part of the Holy Cross family in those days can forget "Rocks?" A man who embodied the spirit of Holy Cross, a man who, I believe, was the most popular man on campus, a blind man who was the envy of us all because of the very attractive and beautiful women who came to campus to read to him, a blind man who stood before a student-packed Kimball Hall, on the eve of a game with Syracuse University, and fired our imaginations and blazed a torchlight parade, the likes of which have not been seen since, with the now famous words, "If you can't find the way, I'll show you!"

Yes, "Rocks" Gallagher was a leader – student manager of the Holy Cross 1947 NCAA Basketball Champions, First Vice President of his 1948 graduating class, and an elected member of Alpha Sigma Nu, the National Jesuit Honor Society, President and Executive Director of the American Foundation for the Blind, Consultant to Hollywood film stars playing roles of blind characters in the movie industry; a provider of generous and effective service to the blind community of the world as a member of the U.S. Delegation to the World Council for the Welfare of the Blind, a gubernatorial appointee to the Board of the New York State Commission for the Blind and Visually Handicapped, a two term President of the Massachusetts Council for Organization of the Blind, and a worker on behalf of the New York Association for the Blind, the Greater Pittsburgh Guild for the Blind, and the Catholic Guild for all the Blind.

Yes, "Rocks" Gallagher, a social worker par excellence, who admirably spent nearly his entire adulthood in the service of those burdened with impaired vision.

"Rocks" Gallagher was a brave, courageous and heroic man – a friend who loved as God loves, who was just and fair, and who throughout his days lived in a state of friendship with God. May the soul of this loyal and admirable Crusader, an honorary member of the Holy Cross Varsity Club Hall of Fame now rest in the peace

Rocks: The Blind Guy at the Lake

of our Risen Lord!

****

Helen Keller was asked: "Is blindness the worst tragedy that can befall a man, woman or child?" She answered that question by saying: "No, The worst loss that a person can suffer is not a loss of sight, but a loss of vision."

What is the difference between loss of sight and loss of vision?

Father Kevin M. Cusick explained the distinction this way:

"To be satisfied only with vision afforded by our eyes is a joy that can become a limitation. There is a blindness more tragic than to be denied the gift of physical sight. And that, of course, is a loss of vision."

We pay homage to and honor people who have:

Humility; Gratitude; Intelligence;

Love for their neighbors;

Feed the hungry; Give drink to the thirsty; Clothe the naked;

Visit the sick and the prisoners; Bury the dead;

Care for the widow and the orphan;

Do not steal; Do not bear false witness against their neighbors; Do not commit adultery;

Love God above all things

A man who has physical sight may have none of these attributes. Such a man is without vision.

A blind man may have some or all of these attributes because he has vision.

William F. Gallagher did not have the gift of sight. He had

something far more valuable. He had the gift of vision – vision to love his fellow man.

Let that be his epitaph.

ADDENDA

....

IRISH AMERICA

Irish America is a nationally known magazine which is published monthly. Its motto is *Mortas Cine – Pride in Our Heritage.*

In its March issue, 1991, it chose its annual list of "Top 100." This list includes the best and brightest from all walks of life, who have some Irish blood coursing through their veins; political, business, church, labor community, sports and entertainment.

The list for the year of 1991 includes

people who have contributed greatly to the community.

Bill Gallagher was one of those chosen among the "Top 100." The entry on Bill is as follows:

WILLIAM GALLAGHER

Blind since his teens, the American Foundation for the Blind's president and executive director, brings to his job a love of people, a drive to excel and above all, a commitment to helping all blind people to live independently and with dignity. Born and raised in Maynard, Massachusetts, he was a normally-sighted 15-year old interested in high school sports when he suffered damage to his optic nerves and became blind overnight. With strong family support, Gallagher finished high school and received a four-year scholarship to Holy Cross College. He is married to the former Catherine O'Brien, an associate professor of nursing at Manhattan Community College and resides in New York City.

****

POSSIBLE CAUSE OF BILL'S BLINDNESS

It was never medically or otherwise determined what caused Bill Gallagher to become totally blind overnight, when he was fifteen years of age.

Rocks: The Blind Guy at the Lake

There was an article in the <u>New York Times</u> in their *Science Times Section*, dated March 29, 2005 which might cast some light on a possible cause of how it all happened.

The article, in part, by Denise Grady is as follows:

SANFORD, Calif. – Kathleen Young had no reason to believe she was anything but healthy. She led a hectic life, running a tree-trimming business with her husband, studying to become a nurse and bringing up three daughters, ages 10, 12 and 13, in Raymore, Mo.

But in an instant last September, everything changed. While working out at the gym, Ms. Young, 41, suddenly went blind in her left eye. Minutes later, it had began to pound. The diagnosis, after an M.R.I. and other tests, was almost beyond comprehension: a rare disease had created blockages in arteries deep inside her skull, cutting off blood flow to part of her brain and causing a stroke, which had partly blinded her.

The disorder, called moyamoya disease, is so uncommon that her family doctor admitted he had never heard of it. The name is Japanese for puff of smoke, which is what the disease looks like on X-rays; a wispy cloud of fragile blood vessels that develop in the brain where normal vessels are blocked. It was first identified in Japan in 1999.

Rocks: The Blind Guy at the Lake

When Ms. Young looked it up, what she learned was devastating. The disease causes a progressive narrowing of the internal carotid arteries, which carry blood to the brain. Patients suffer multiple strokes, mental decline and, usually death from brain hemorrhage. The cause is unknown, and there is no cure. Reading a textbook chapter on it, she was stunned to realize that much of the information came from autopsies.

It should be noted that this information was not available until 1955, long after Bill was blinded.

****

TWENTY LOSSES (from *Carroll's thesis was that an adult who becomes blind loses not only sight but also loses 20 specific things related to it)*

LOSS OF PHYSICAL SECURITY

The first bitter blow in the multiple handicap of blindness is loss of physical integrity, of wholeness. The person who grew up, who built his life as a whole person, is now only a part. He is shattered.

The blind person must drastically revise the body image which he had of himself when he was sighted. Now, he must drastically revise that image. His body is a blind and maimed body – a windowless, abnormal body. What happens to his equilibrium, to his whole method of action?" wrote Carroll.

One of the effects of this state of mind is the new insecurity about his manhood.

LOSS OF CONFIDENCE IN THE REMAINING SENSES

Do blinded people have an acuteness of the remaining senses, such as sighted people never know? Carroll suggests that sighted people should disabuse themselves of such a notion. He states:

> It comes as a surprise to learn that new blindness can cause a loss of confidence in the remaining senses. This loss of confidence is not the result of that actual destruction of the sense of sense function.

The loss comes about basically because the blinded individual does not trust what his remaining senses tell him.

Carroll sums up this segment by stating: This loss particularly during the shock-stage of new blindness, is a shattering one, since it leaves a man so completely helpless. It removes him further from the world about him and makes more distant the possibility of rehabilitation."

LOSS OF REALITY CONTACT WITH ENVIRONMENT

"The loss of contact with reality of 'reality contact' with the tangible world in which we live, is one that easily leads to panic or that makes still more numb the numbness of the stage of shock. It's a further 'death' to the world of things about us" writes Carroll.

Carroll illustrates his point:

> . . . *it is sight above all which fixes me in my relationship to things around me. Sight relates me to the things to right and to left, to things above and below, to things in front of me and even in back of me. Sight not only identifies these things, it centers me among them.*

He concludes that this loss is "one of the most frightening aspects of the multiple trauma of blindness."

LOSS OF VISUAL BACKGROUND

Carroll makes a distinction of seeing an object and seeing an object against a background. On a subway, for example, we see not only the person opposite us, but we also see the structure of the train itself, the station, the platform, different colors, etc. These other things are observed subconsciously. Carroll describes this loss of background as "visual silence."

LOSS OF LIGHT SECURITY

It is Carroll's contention that speaking of blindness as a "loss of light" is inaccurate. He explains: "Light is medium for sight. It is not sight itself. If the medium is absent, or if it is present in too great a quantity, we are unable to make use of it. But the medium is not the sense, light is not sight."

"The definition most commonly accepted of blindness in the United States is an equivalent of the following: A person shall be considered blind whose central acuity does not exceed 20/200 in the better eye with correcting lenses, or whose visual acuity is greater than 20/200, but is accompanied by a limitation in the fields of vision, such as the widest diameter of the visual field subtends an angle of no greater than 20 degrees."

To phrase it another way, Carroll states: "These people are clearly blind, yet they are not without light." He points out that light in our society has positive connotations - truth, beauty, goodness. On the other hand, darkness has negative connotations – evil, crime, sin, the shadow of death. For this reason, for society to say that a blind person lives in a world of darkness, is to place an unfair burden on him, as he tries to fully integrate himself into society.

LOSS OF MOBILITY

According to Carroll, a person who suddenly loses sight is immobilized. This loss of mobility is a major loss, one of the greatest reality losses which follow the loss of sight.

LOSS OF TECHNIQUES OF DAILY LIVING

"The little things – maddening in their inconvenience – eating and drinking, caring for bowel and bladder functions, keeping oneself clean and neat, undressing at night and dressing in the morning."

Carroll offers a simple example – try eating blindfolded. Think of every little act you must perform during the day and think of how a blind man handles each and everyone, e.g., you drop your key on the floor. Now you have to find it without sight.

LOSS OF EASE OF WRITTEN COMMUNICATION

"The greatest loss in this connection is the loss of the ability to read one's own mail with the corresponding loss of the ability to write one's own letters, to keep up one's personal correspondence without intrusion of another party. Those losses may be painful because they involve not only independence but personal privacy."

LOSS OF EASE OF SPOKEN COMMUNICATION

"This loss effects not only actual listening and speaking, but also gestures, posture, mannerisms, pantomimes and facial expression – all the unspoken elements of "spoken" communication."

People who speak may shrug their shoulders, arch their eye brows, toss their heads "which in themselves are word phrases or sentences and sometimes, more important than many worded speeches."

Consider how great the loss is to the blind person. He says something serious or funny, but he cannot read the other person's reaction.

LOSS OF INFORMATIONAL PROGRESS

"This loss might be given various names: loss of awareness of the social scene, loss of growth in information, loss of ability to keep up with the times, or loss of contact with the present day. It is a loss of progress when other things are moving on, or standing still while the world goes by, in fact, a moving backward, since it puts the blinded person far behind his previous position."

Father Carroll points out that "progress here depends in great part on two things – on reaching and on the observation of people and things."

One of the negative aspects of lack of

current information may lead his acquaintances "to think of the blinded person's lack of current information as stupidity."

LOSS OF THE VISUAL PERCEPTION OF THE PLEASURABLE

Father Carroll gives an example of this loss when he speaks of the reaction "of those who have regained their sight after years of blindness." They may say something like: "The most wonderful thing was to see my wife and children . . . or for the first time in years, I saw the house I have lived in so long."

LOSS OF VISUAL PERCEPTION OF THE BEAUTIFUL

For those who have a strong love of the beautiful and become blinded, "it is a loss so keen and close to the heart that to speak of it in the wrong words to the wrong people, would cheapen and sully its meaning and would be worse than nothing."

LOSS OF RECREATION

Recreation is an important facet of every day life. Carroll explains this loss as it affects the blinded person: "In one or another form, it is important to everybody, most of all to those under serious stress. Yet in the midst of new blindness with all the stresses and strains it brings about, the blind man has lost recreation also. From any standpoint, this is a major loss."

LOSS OF CAREER VOCATIONAL GOAL, JOB OPPORTUNITY

Carroll points out that this loss and its impact vary with each individual. However, for every such person "who would normally be working, the loss of job opportunity, of vocational goal, the closing out of a career, is in itself, a severe loss, and should be recognized as such. The 'death' here is to usefulness to a life of productivity and worth."

LOSS OF PERSONAL INDEPENDENCE

Carroll explains: "Every loss that we have been considering involves a loss of independence – even the loss of physical integrity, for one of the first feelings it brings with it, is that of being a dependent person, and the very fact of being 'different,' makes dependency more difficult to accept."

Carroll offers this insightful statement: "Bur the measure of true maturity and of true independence is the degree to which we can accept dependence when it is forced on us."

"The terrible loss of personal independence is, then, one of the most significant losses which the multiple handicap of blindness entails – since death to independence means an end to adult living."

LOSS OF SOCIAL ADEQUACY

This is "one of the most serious blows

which blindness deals to the average person."
On this revelation, Carroll admonishes the
public: "We, the sighted public, add this extra
loss to the multiple handicap of blindness
because we are afraid of blindness – of all the
connotations of blindness – all the dark, evil,
ignorance and mystery involved in shadow and
gloom."

One of the saddest effects that sighted
people have on the blinded is their
condescending attitudes towards the blinded, e.g.,
"It's amazing how happy they (the blinded) are.
Or isn't it amazing how they can tell colors."

This often leads the blinded person to feel
"that he is no longer accepted for himself."
Father Carroll sums this up:

> We fear blindness, we sighted
> people. And we cannot meet the
> emotions and feelings it arouses
> within us sufficiently to give the
> blind person his personal place
> among us. We cannot, that is,
> until we are willing to face
> ourselves and our feelings and to
> treat blind men (and women)
> according to their individual
> worth and their human dignity.

LOSS OF OBSCURITY

The blind man "is subject to the glaring

light in which public figures must live, but unlike so many public figures, he has not sought it; he has been forced into it by the fact of his blindness. Not only is he living in a show window (with a glass through which he is seen, but cannot see), but he is expected to 'conform' to a degree not demanded of the average person."

A sighted man is easily lost in a crowd. The blind man is not. Carroll sums it up this way: "The loss of obscurity, in which is interwoven a loss of individuality, is a severe and continuing trauma for the individual who loses sight – a trauma in which his privacy dies."

LOSS OF SELF ESTEEM
Carroll's observed, "Within us, then, there are two different estimates of self – the intellectual evaluation or objective self-estimate. . . ; and the reflection of all the thinking and feeling we did about ourselves as children and whatever growth has come to it, since our "Feeling self evaluation" or "self image."

Concerning objective self image, the blinded person may think along these lines: "He was a whole person; now he is maimed. He was sure of his manhood; now he has gnawing doubts – he cannot trust his remaining senses. . . In a life of lightlessness, he is alone and not sure of love. . . He has dropped in his status in the community, has had a secondary role forced on him in his family; he has almost lost his individuality and is no longer accepted for himself alone. His objective self evaluation has received a shattering blow. To accept this blow, may well mean that he must begin his life again from the start."

With respect to the blind person's self image, Carroll states: ". . . in a sense everyone's balance in life consists in his establishing an equilibrium with his self image"

Carroll also discusses "the anxiety that may arise in many newly blinded persons when it has never been a problem before; it may be with them until they die unless with psychiatric help, they are able to bring it under control."

Carroll finishes this section of his book by stating:

> *The last great blow of blindness is the blow which this multiple traumatic experience exercises upon the total personality organization. Putting the pieces back together, mending this blow, is the greatest challenge to agencies for the blind. For here, the very personality has suffered a death.*

****

SCHOOLS AND COLLEGES

WORCESTER TELEGRAM

9 H.C. Students Named to Jesuit Honor Society

Nine Holy Cross College students have been elected to the Alpha Sigma NU, National Jesuit Honor Society, Rev. Joseph D. Fitzgerald, S.J., Dean, announced yesterday.

Junior members are: Roy W. Riel, member of Cross and Scroll Society; William Gallagher, the blind "good luck charm" of the basketball team and member of the Purple Key; Thomas P. Costello, member of the BFJ Debating Society and John J. Donohue, Purple Key member.

Members are elected on a basis of all-around ability, which includes scholarship and extra-curricular activity.

Worcester Telegram

****

Rocks: The Blind Guy at the Lake

THE PATRIOT

June 5, 1991

Gallagher Retires to Bates Point

WEBSTER – William F. Gallagher is now making Bates Point Road his year-round home.

He retired recently from his position of President and Executive Director of the American Foundation for the Blind in New York City.

For 20 years he considered Webster his second home.

Born in Maynard, he was 15 years old when he literally overnight became blind. After two years, doctors were forced to admit that the damage to his optic nerves from whatever the source seemed to be permanent. He then enrolled in the nearby Perkins School for the Blind in Watertown in 1941.

There, he became President of the Student Council and Athletic Association, Captain of the Wrestling Team and Members of the Drama and Debating Societies.

It was there that he met the Rev. Thomas J. Carroll, who was Director of the Catholic Guild for all the Blind. The priest was an influence in Gallagher deciding to attend Holy Cross College in Worcester. Then he received a two-year scholarship from the Boston College School of Social Work.

Rocks: The Blind Guy at the Lake

After working as a social worker in the child welfare department for Boston, he accepted an invitation from Father Carroll with the St. Paul's Rehabilitation Center for the Newly Blinded at the Catholic Guild for All the Blind in Newtown. After working for the Greater Pittsburgh Guild for the Blind and the New York Association for the Blind, he joined the American Foundation for the Blind in 1965. He advanced in that organization to being president and executive director in 1989 until his retirement.

Now, he will work three days a week with the Perkins School as a consultant.

His many honors include the Founders Award from the Massachusetts Council of Organization for the Blind, 1960; a citation as Citizen of the Week in Pittsburgh in 1962; a citation from the National Rehabilitation Association from New York in 1971; the George Keane Award from the New York State Chapter, American Association for Workers for the Blind in 1974 for 20 years of outstanding work in providing services to the blind; recipient of Greater Pittsburgh Guild for the Blind 1982 President's Award in 1982; recipient of Association for Education of the Visually Handicapped 1982 Presidential Award in 1982; recipient of Distinguished Service Award of the President's Committee on Employment of the Handicapped in 1985; recipient of the Francis Joseph Campbell Citation and Medal for contributions to the advancement of library service to the blind from the American Library Association in 1987; recipient of the Carel C. Koch Memorial Medal from the American Academy of Optometry in 1987; recipient of the C. Stanley Potter Award of the National Association of Radio Reading Services from the Association of Radio Reading Services in 1990 and the recipient of the Peter J. Salmon Memorial Award from the American Association of the Deaf-Blind in 1990.

He has written numerous articles and chapters on education, rehabilitation and social work. Most recently his paper, "Categorical Services in the Age of Integration: Paradox or Contradiction" was a principal presentation at an international symposium held in Melbourne, Australia.

He is an avid follower of collegiate basketball and professional football and baseball, especially the Boston Red Sox. He enjoys boating, fishing and swimming.

In March, he was named one of the *Top 100* by the publication Irish America.

****

Rocks: The Blind Guy at the Lake

HIS VOICE

     This poem, <u>His Voice</u>, was recited at the unveiling of a plaque installed in Rocks' honor at the Hogan Campus Center, Holy Cross College on October 13, 2001.

Men of the Class of
'48

Be at ease

I have passed
through the

Pearly Gate

Long days ago

I want each of you
to

Know

That I see you right
there

Before me

In the light of this
memorable

Day

Homecoming is always
such a

Rocks: The Blind Guy at the Lake

Special time

What wondrous
memories of

This day are mine

St. Peter gave me a special
pass

For the game

I'll be sitting on the
Crusader

Bench

On the 50 yard line

If you look hard
enough

You will see me
sitting there

Beside my bride so
sweet and

Fair

So lift your glasses
high

Raise your voices
to the sky

And give another
Hoya and

A Choo Choo Rah
Rah

Rocks: The Blind Guy at the Lake

For the boys on
Fitton Field

The Purple Banner
they

Will not yield

Let there be heard

This one final word

From the depths of
my heart

I thank each one of
you

For the memory of
this day

Never has a man
had friends

So tried and so
true.

Thomas Costello

****

Rocks: The Blind Guy at the Lake

New York Times
May 1, 2000, Monday

NATIONAL DESK

W.F. GALLAGHER, 77 Dies; Led Foundation for Blind

By WOLFGANG SAXON (Obituary (Obit); Biography; 478 words)

William Gallagher, a retired president of the American Foundation for the Blind, died on April 19 at his home in Webster, Massachusetts, south of Worcester. He was 77 and had long been ill, said the Foundation, based in Manhattan, where Mr. Gallagher formerly lived on the Upper East Side.

Mr. Gallagher, who lost his own sight in boyhood, joined the staff of the Foundation in 1972 as director of program planning and as such oversaw policies carried out by regional branches stretching from New York to San Francisco and advised on matters like fund-raising, public relations and research objectives.

He was named associate director for advocacy in 1978, managing field services, government relations, publications, conferences, workshops and training sessions. He advanced to executive director in 1980, added the title of president in 1989 and retired the next year.

The Foundation, which in addition to serving the blind preserves the archives of Helen

Rocks: The Blind Guy at the Lake

Keller, the organization's principal fund-raiser and adviser in the 1950's, credits Mr. Gallagher with having kept staff and trustees abreast of the needs of the blind by establishing national advisory boards of leaders in education, rehabilitation and aging. It says he also helped improve standards for the accreditation of specialized schools and agencies that offer services to the 10 million Americans who are blind or have limited sight.

William Gallagher was born in Maynard, Massachusetts, near Boston, and graduated from the Perkins School for the Blind in Watertown, Massachusetts, where he was President of the Student Council, President of the Athletic Association, Captain of the Wrestling Team and a Member of the Debating Society. He graduated from Holy Cross with a degree in sociology in 1948 and received a master's in social work at Boston College in 1950.

He started 40 years of service to the blind that year as a children's social worker for the City of Boston and for the Catholic Guild for All the Blind in Newton, Massachusetts. He then worked at rehabilitation centers in Newton and in Bridgeville, Pennsylvania and in 1965 was named director of rehabilitation services for the New York Lighthouse.

Rocks: The Blind Guy at the Lake

****

---

[i] Blindism - ism - manner of action characteristic of a specified person & characteristic or peculiar feature or trait from <u>Websters</u>.

[ii] *Writer's Interpretation of the meaning of those words: The passing parade was the going from and coming back of the veterans of World War II.*

[iii] Keymen: There was an organization on the Hill (Holy Cross) known as the Purple Key...a greeting Committee for new students.

Made in the USA
Lexington, KY
02 April 2012